For Sales' Sake Meditate!

Join the New Breed of Supersalesmen
Because You Won't Beat Them!

Vincent J. Daczynski

HATS
OFF

For Sales' Sake Meditate!

International Standard Book Number: 1-58736-119-1
Library of Congress Card Number: 2002092660

Published by Hats Off Books™

610 East Delano Street, Suite 104, Tucson, Arizona 85705, U.S.A.
www.hatsoffbooks.com

Front cover: Tarantula Nebula in our galactic neighbor, the Large Magellanic Cloud. NASA, The Hubble Heritage Team (STScI/AURA) and Y. H. Chu (U. Illinois)

®Transcendental Meditation, TM, TM-Sidhi, Science of Creative Intelligence, Age of Enlightenment, World Plan, Maharishi Corporate Development Program, Maharishi Sthāpatya Veda, Maharishi Effect, Maharishi University of Management are registered or common law trademarks licensed to Maharishi Vedic Educational Development Corporation.

Cartoon on p. 97 by Paul Carlson.

This book is written with deepest gratitude to His Holiness Maharishi Mahesh Yogi for lifting me out of the tumultuous vicissitudes of life with a simple technique of meditation, giving me inner peace, happiness and success. And in memory of my mentors and dearest friends, Helen and Charlie Lutes, for their continued guidance and inspiration.

All proceeds from the sale of this book are donated to Maharishi Vedic Education Development Corporation and its associated organizations in order to share with others what I have gained from the simple truths expressed in this book.

JOIN THE NEW BREED OF SUPERSALESMEN
BECAUSE YOU WON'T BEAT THEM!

The sales training concepts presented in this book are supported by over 600 research studies conducted at more than 200 universities and research institutions in 33 countries, and published in more than 100 major scientific journals.

Table of Contents

Table of Contents

Author's Note

This work is contrary to many other schools of thought in sales training that I openly challenge. I do some stepping on toes, but not out of mischievous intent. Only that I need to draw a firm comparison between this system of sales training and all other systems. And I do so out of my conviction that the following text is the most advanced school of thought available today for training salesmen.

I particularly call your attention to the overwhelming supporting scientific data referenced throughout this book. This scientific data points to a major breakthrough in developing human potential.

This book reads much as a lecture because it was gleaned from lecture notes I used when making presentations to sales training classes. The receptivity I received, and the growing acceptance among corporations of this system of training, led me to expand my lecture notes into this comprehensive text.

I sincerely hope that this book serves to open your awareness to a broadened understanding of human potential and its development.

Preface

Since its introduction to the Western world fifty years ago, the Transcendental Meditation (TM) technique as a means of personal development has been the subject of over 600 scientific research studies conducted at 200 independent universities and research institutions in thirty-three countries. These studies have been published in such leading journals as the *Academy of Management Journal, American Journal of Physiology, American Journal of Psychiatry, Hypertension, The Lancet, Science,* and *Scientific American.* No other system of personal development has received such scrutiny and acclaim.

The scientific data echo the personal experiences of over five million practitioners of the TM technique, including people of all ages, professions, cultures and religions throughout the world. A renewed understanding of human development is unfolding. I state *renewed* because the TM technique is not something new that has been developed or contrived.

Only its name is new. *Transcendental Meditation* is a coined term for an ancient teaching dating back to the earliest records of human experience. It is a sacred science which heretofore has been reverently guarded and imparted by a teacher, on a one-on-one basis, to only the most trusted, favored and zealous students.

Maharishi Mahesh Yogi, the founder and the inspirational leader of the world-wide TM movement, has broken the exclusive tradition and brought this ancient teaching to the mundane world in response to the demands of the tumultuous times in which we live.

This book explores this ancient teaching in light of its application to the sales profession. The first part of the book provides an introduction and orientation to the essence of the wise teachings and shows how this essence is the single key required to unlock the holistic unfoldment of the salesman. After providing the basic understanding, Part II discusses how, through the practice of the TM-Sidhi program, people can accelerate their development towards unfolding a state of consciousness called *cosmic consciousness,* or *enlightenment.*

Simply reading this book will not enable you to achieve this status. The critical instruction, the TM technique, must be imparted on a personal level by a specially trained instructor. However, personal instruction is readily available. There is a team of over 10,000 teachers available at 350 centers across the United States alone. There are 40,000 teachers throughout the democratic world.

Mind is the ultimate frontier and contains the greatest potential power. The purpose of this book is to introduce a system of personal development which can unfold the full utilization of your mental potential to a superhuman status.

Already, many internationally renowned corporations have taken advantage of the ancient teachings described in this text by implementing Transcendental Meditation programs for their executives and employees. It behooves you to learn about this most advanced method available for self-development. If you are not already competing against it, you will be!

Part I

Introduction and Orientation

The Transcendental Meditation
Program

Chapter I

What in the Name of Sales?

Over the last thirty-five years I have been through several sales training programs in real estate, insurance and securities. Additionally, I have read and studied numerous books on selling and psychology and I have reviewed many self-improvement courses. And as a consumer, I have been at the receiving end of a wide variety of sales presentations. I discovered that all sales training follows a central theme utilizing variations of one or more of the following: manipulation, gimmicks, ploys, showmanship, deception, control, dominance, psychological game playing, word mongering and canned pitches. Basically, selling today is taught in terms of staging a performance. However, the 'sales act' technique has run its course and is not apropos for the times in which we are living.

Buyers today are far more aware. They have increased product knowledge and understand themselves and others a lot better than they did a decade ago. Buyers know a put-on when they see it and are quick to spot insincerity. Until recently, most people have accepted the 'sales performance' as part of a game which had to be played if they wanted to acquire any goods and services. Now, people are tired of playing games. They have too many problems on their minds. Corporate downsizing and mergers leading to layoffs and downgrades, and just general economic uncertainty, are forcing people to do with a lot less. Today, it is much easier for the purchasing agent or the housewife to say, "No!" The sales actor looking for a stage upon which to do his act invites a hasty brush-off. But the show must go on. The salesman must perform. Sales trainers and sales managers, themselves graduates of the 'salesman school of performing arts' perpetuate the folly by their mandate of how products and services must be sold. What should be a professional show-and-tell based on a natural wholesome sincere communication between individuals, instead, is being played in terms of manipulation, even deception, with some salesmen using every conceivable tactic short of drawing a gun to make the sale. I will cite a few examples to illustrate this point.

During my sales training as a stockbroker, I was told a story about a pro-football player who became a salesman. After making a number of personal cold calls to businesses, he soon discovered that his rugged, mesomorphic appearance and size overwhelmed receptionists. This caused resistance in the receptionists, making it difficult for him to get their cooperation in permitting him to see the key individuals.

So he devised a tactic; he would trip and fall, scattering his papers on the floor, as he approached the receptionist's desk. By feigning a fall he would bring out the heartfelt sympathetic emotions of the receptionist, quickly melting her resistance. Oftentimes the receptionist would help him pick up his papers, and within moments they became friends. This ploy would get the empathic receptionist working on the salesman's side, opening doors to key individuals for him.

When I was attending a major insurance company's sales training orientation program in Connecticut, during the morning coffee break, the speaker sneaked up behind one of the group members and bellowed out a mighty lion-like roar, nearly scaring the guy to death. The six-and-a-half-foot speaker was the product of this company's advanced motivation training program.

"We can't tell you all of what we do in our advanced sales training courses," he boasted later to the class. "But our salesmen break chairs, desks, and one guy rammed his fist one-inch into a solid plaster wall. When we get finished with you, you will be aggressive, motivated, domineering, and you will sell!"

Sell? Why not issue blackjacks? This company runs a boot camp-type of program. They teach dominance and aggressiveness, and direct that aroused energy towards selling. It is interesting to note that this insurance company has higher rates than most of their competitors. With the goon squad they develop for making high pressure sales they do not need competitive pricing.

I also attended real estate sales training classes in San Francisco conducted by a major land developer. I was pitched the following line at the opening of every class, "I am going to teach you how to take money out of other peoples' pockets and put it in your pocket where it belongs." What was this, a school for training pickpockets?

A computer leasing firm in New York City used this outrageous technique for closing deals. "Mr. X, you have nothing to lose. Exercise your option to buy your computer equipment from the manufacturer. We will in turn buy the equipment from you at the same price you paid. Then, we will lease the equipment back to you for 30% less than you now pay. And as an added incentive we are prepared to rebate the first two month's rental payment. Ahh ... Mr. X, we do not care who the rebate check is made payable to." At that point the sure-fire salesman hands Mr. X an endorsed check, with the payee section blank, and a contract to sign. This procedure was used by a major national computer leasing company as a standard procedure to build their empire. The ends never justify the means!

Some twenty years ago, when I was preparing to give a lecture on the TM program, I rented a meeting room for the occasion. Coincidentally, the adjacent meeting room was rented by the "Dare to be Great" self-help pyramid marketing group. I arrived early and so did their speaker. He noticed me and targeted me for a pitch. His first maneuver was to show me his identification card proving himself to be a minister. "No reason why one should not make some money while helping his fellow man," he stated. Once he realized that I was the scheduled speaker in the adjacent room, which had only an accordion-type sliding door as a partition, he stated that he hoped that his group would not disturb me. "We make a lot of noise," he said several times during our conversation. "We holler and scream and stomp our feet," he said. He was right. They made a lot of noise. In fact, so much noise that Blue Sky securities laws were re-written in many states.

Here is another example. I was out with my family looking for residential property. We were being ushered to the property by a realtor who had an interesting exclusive listing on a must-see-to-appreciate property that was sure to sell fast, etc. En route, the realtor casually pointed out the various properties that he had sold. Ironically, as we passed a twenty-nine-unit apartment house, which I happened to live in, he pointed to it stating that he had sold that property the prior year. The truth was, I sold it! The apartment manager had told me that the owners were planning on selling. I knew of a buyer and got a finder's fee for bringing together the principles. You can imagine the dialogue that followed. Why the need for lying? I subsequently found a realtor whom I could trust and bought my house with her help.

Another salesman I encountered was pushing a course in personal development and tried this tactic for closing the sale. He obnoxiously yelled commands at me, "Sign the contract! Sign the contract!" as he pounded his finger at the dotted line. Did he ever figure me wrongly!

Here is another example of my sales training with a securities firm. The vice president of this national brokerage house related the following tactic to me which he used to pick up customers.

> I walk down the street keeping an eye open for possibilities. One day, for example, I saw a machine shop door open with some heavy equipment operating inside the shop. I stood outside intently watching the equipment. I figured that sooner or later someone is going to notice me and ask me what I am doing. Sure enough, the manager walked over and asked if he could help me with something. I told him, 'Oh, no. Watching heavy machinery, like that operating, always fascinates me.' And we get to talking. Get the idea? In time he will ask you what you do for a living. You have to reply real easy, casual, somewhat incidental, and incomplete; something like, 'investments.' Do not tell him that you are a stockbroker. Your reply will build curiosity and naturally will draw him to ask what kind of investments you are into. Keep tantalizing him to keep him coming. Eventually, he will ask you for your business card. But don't carry business cards. If you give him a card, it's all over—he will probably never call you. Tell him that you are out of cards. This gives you the opportunity to get his name and to follow-up with a note, at which time you include a card.

The vice president, who was my boss, told me he used variations of this approach wherever he happened to be: fishing, shopping, playing golf, etc. He tried hard, but could not indoctrinate me to his style. To me this type of selling approach is two-faced, and reminds me of a saying, "There are people in this world who can pat you on the back with one hand while they pick your pocket with the other."

As if these types of sales methods are not bad enough, some people go to the extremes of using subliminal mind control and various occult methods in order to obtain sales. What in the name of sales? Why do some salesmen feel it is necessary to go to such extremes in order to succeed in selling?

The key to being a professional salesman is being natural, being yourself. If you have to put on an act or use ploys to sell you are either in the wrong business, or you need to unfold your natural inner self. Selling comes naturally to the professional salesman. Yes, it takes hard work. But what accounts for the fact that 20% of the salesmen make 80% of the sales? And why is this success continual regardless of outside circumstances, territories, leads, business conditions, competition, the economy, etc.? How can you acquire what the successful salesmen have, and how can you duplicate and surpass their success? What is it that successful salesmen have going for them that others do not have? The answer lies in understanding what the root cause of success is. The basic ingredient for success has been known for centuries. Nevertheless, sales managers and trainers, in trying to close the gap between their top performers and the rest of their sales staff (not to mention the gap with outside competition) resort to psychological game playing, manipulating the psyche of their salesmen via a variety of positive-thinking-type inspirational and motivational courses to program the right mood for the planned staged performances. To this is added an ever growing spiral of gimmicks and psychological sales paraphernalia. Further, salesmen are conditioned for robot-like responses designed for quick psychological victory over the customer being served. And this is called *professional* sales training. As you read this book you will realize the shortcomings of today's sales training methods. More importantly, you will discover that you can become a supersalesman without the use of theatrics, psychological programming, or client manipulations.

Chapter II

Positive Thinking Is Not Enough

Numerous books, cassette tapes and courses have been produced that utilize the positive thinking method for achieving success. Because of the widespread use of this type of approach to personal development and achieving success, I have devoted an entire chapter to its analysis.

All positive thinking methodologies are based on the philosophy that if you think positive, you will be positive. From this premise a variety of pep talk and self-hypnosis type of inspirational and motivational courses have evolved.

It is my conviction that this premise of thinking positive in order to be positive is wrong, and therefore, will produce limited results. Being positive does not result from thinking positive. Thinking positive comes from being positive. The effect comes from the cause and not vice versa. I realize that I must be stepping on a lot of toes, but follow along with me for a while as I develop this theme and you will discover the shortcoming in the positive thinking approach to achieving success. Certainly, benefits have been experienced from positive thinking programs. However, when positive thinking is not natural, but forced, the results, at best, will be limited, temporary, and self-deluding. It is like putting the cart before the horse. Some progress may be made. However, a broader perspective of the mechanics of progress will conclude that maximum progress will be made when the horse is placed before the cart. Similarly, we must first be positive and then we will think positive. So *being* precedes *thinking*. And thinking is the basis for action. Before you can act there must be some thought impulse. *Thinking* precedes *action*. Effective thinking will yield effective action. First *being*, then *thinking*, then *action* – this is the sequence for maximum success. This will become more obvious as you read Chapter III.

Again, positive behavior, i.e., effective action, results from positive thinking, and positive thinking results from being positive. See Fig. 1.

Sequence for Maximum Success

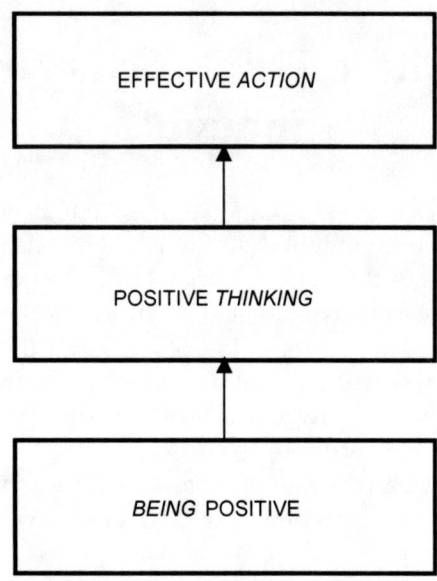

Fig. 1. First *Being*, then *Thinking*, then *Action* is the sequence for maximum success

We begin to see the key to success and the method to achieve it. We must transcend the level of positive thinking and *be* positive. Positive thinking will thereby occur in a natural, spontaneous manner; it will not be a contrived mood-making mental manipulation.

In 1973, I attended a seminar in San Francisco conducted by one of the leading developers of positive-thinking-type sales development programs. The president of the company gave the pitch, and I must say that I was very impressed with this eloquent speaker, whose stage-presence and charisma gave him a command and magnetism that itself induced me to want what he had to sell. After listening to him for a while I concluded that he exemplified everything that his sales development course was said to achieve. But how did he get that way? How did he gain his positive attitude and success? By listening to pep talks on cassettes? No. He probably never had to listen to pep talks, because he was already drawing from that level of *being* positive, whether he realized that fact or not. And how did he draw from that level of *being* positive? He was either born with that depth of mental ability, or he gained that ability as part of his maturing process. Successful people operate from that inner level of *being. And the greater the contact is with that inner being, the greater is the success.* But positive thinking, as has been brought out earlier, will not connect you to *being* positive. And unless you are connected and live your life from that *being* positive level, the best you can expect to accomplish from positive thinking is an imitation of being positive. Positive thinking, pep talks, telling yourself that you are terrific, or that you are a successful salesman, etc., is deluding.

An actor believes himself to be someone that he is not. He assumes the role of, say, a king or ruler, and then plays the role. But when the filming ends, who is the actor? Is he the king? No, it's back to being himself. Many actors feel frustrated by not being able to measure up to the image they portray. I am sure that the same is true of many salesmen today. During filming, the actor has to be very attentive to how and where he stands, how he makes every motion, and how he says his lines. He has a wide range of variables which he must consider and manipulate to perform just right. If he makes an error, however, it is no big problem since the director is there to assist him through the retake. And even after the filming there is the editing which can compensate for errors that might have been made.

The salesman is faced with just as many variables to contend with as is the actor. He must work within widely differing markets and customers. He must blend his personal attributes and abilities harmoniously within many varied selling situations and different personalities. However, he does not get a second chance at it. The salesman who is naturally being positive does not need to think of psyching himself up any more than a real king has to put attention on being a king. It is not possible to effectively handle the wide range of variables with which a salesman is confronted through rehearsals or by hyping up the salesman via positive-thinking-type inspirational and motivational programs. But isn't this what today's sales training programs try to accomplish?

Getting back to the sales seminar I attended: After the company president spoke, his assistant made a speech. It was well delivered, but, there was an obvious difference between his presentation and that of the president. All gestures and speech inflections appeared contrived and forced. He was not operating from the same level as was the president. He was acting, imitating, and trying to be as good as his boss. I, as the potential customer, could sense this. Your customers sense it when you put on an act for them just as easily as you know an act when you see one. The firm's president was natural. He was being himself, and he was terrific. I am sure he felt terrific as a *result* of *being* terrific. The assistant was a poor imitation, although he undoubtedly deluded himself to think that he too was terrific.

A poor man can tell himself that he is rich and get to believe it, but it will not change his poverty, only his mood. In fact, thinking himself to be rich he may not feel the need to do something about his poverty. How many people live in self-deluding fantasies of one type or another? They are like the proverbial ostrich that sticks his head in the sand. His altered perspective brings him comfort. However, others can still see the situation for what it is. A person can be hypnotized not to feel pain. A blowtorch can then be put to him. He might not feel the pain, but damage will certainly result.

I am not against positive thinking. Of course, everyone should think in positive terms. I maintain, however, that positive thinking should have its basis in that deep inner status of *being* positive. Positive thinking should not be a mood that is painted on one's psyche by daily pep talks. That is delusion and operates on the horizontal thinking level of the mind. Sales training programs lack the vertical depth required to enable one to become positive from within himself, be it, and express it from that inner level.

Since the philosophy of positive thinking is incomplete, the results must be incomplete. In order to develop a supersalesman — and *super* means '*totally* developed' — we must have a holistic teaching. And the test of the efficacy of that holistic teaching will be in its ability to develop supersalesmen. The knowledge for the holistic development of the individual is the ancient key to success, dealt with in greater detail in the next chapter.

Chapter III

The Ancient Key to Success

We saw in the previous chapter that positive action, effective success-ful action, is based on positive thinking, and that being positive is the basis for thinking positive. It is *being* that is the underlying basic foun-dation wherein success has its roots. Whether we consider *being* posi-tive, or *being* dynamic, or *being* intelligent, or *being* energetic, or *being* healthy, or *being* happy, or *being* sociable, or *being* anything, we must first *be*. *Being*, existence, that essence of life itself, is that level of life deep within the individual whence all positive creative impulses of life come. *Being* is that primary force that permeates all life. It is infi-nite, unbounded, omnipotent, omniscient, and it is your true inner nature. It is your inner, unlimited storehouse of all possibilities. In itself it is absolute, unchanging. But it is the source, deep within you — it is the infinite, omnipotent and omniscient level — from where all of your aspirations, ambitions, thoughts, etc., arise.

A man is known by his actions. And how he acts is based on how he thinks. And how he thinks is based on the extent to which he is connected to his own inner nature, *being*. Failures, sickness, suffering, social unrest and all negativity are due to lack of knowledge about, and *contact* with, one's own inner nature. It is impossible to be con-nected to the infinite, omnipotent, omniscient level of one's own inner life and be a failure. It is when life is not lived anchored deep in *being* that one is tossed about by the surface waves of life.

I am sure that you recognize that this is not a new teaching. Yet, how many people make use of it in their daily lives? The teaching has always been, "*First* enter the Kingdom of Heaven and then all shall be added unto you." Notice the emphasis on *first*. And where is the Kingdom of Heaven to be found? Is it some mythical place we ascend to after we depart from this earthly plane of existence? No. We are told, "The Kingdom of Heaven lies within." We must first bring our awareness to that level of life deep within us and then perform action. This is the way to acquire success in all areas of life—and *all* means 'all.' Success in all areas of life is a natural by-product resulting from *contacting* that inner *being* (Kingdom of Heaven) within you.

How often have you also heard, "Know Thyself." This is the same teaching. It does not mean to go to a psychoanalyst, or to begin a process of self-inquiry. The *self* is the fountainhead level of life within you. The *self* is that inner universality of life which is your true inner nature. It is *being*. It is that latent inner aspect of your life which is the field of all possibilities.

In the Muslim tradition this truth has been expressed as: "*ana'l-Haqq*" ("I am the Truth"). In the Vedic Literature this truth has been expressed as "*Aham Brahmāsmi*" ("I am the totality").

This truth may be held by some to be a philosophy or a religious doctrine. However, it is also a basic scientific truth. Albeit this truth has been found throughout religious teachings does not make the truth religious. It is a truth apart from the religious doctrines which have upheld it, and it is a truth directly applicable to our selling endeavors.

Quantum mechanics in modern physics identifies a field of life that is analogous to the ancient teachings. It states that there is a ground state, a unified field, which is the fundamental nonchanging field of life. It is eternal, unbounded, beyond space and time, wherein are contained all possibilities. It is the unmanifested field of pure potentiality from where all force and matter fields emerge. If you have this you have everything. Some early physicists have postulated that this unmanifested field of pure potentiality may be consciousness itself. Max Planck stated, "I regard consciousness as fundamental. I regard matter as derivative from consciousness." And Sir Arthur Stanley Eddington said, "All through the physical world runs the unknown content that must surely be the stuff of our consciousness."

Renown Harvard graduate and physicist, Dr. John Hagelin, who is also a qualified teacher of the Transcendental Meditation technique, is spearheading the cutting edge of the recent discovery that a unified field of consciousness is indeed at the foundation of all conscious experience. He argues that consciousness is fundamental in nature— the lively origin and basis of everything in creation—and not merely the result of biochemical processes in the brain. Dr. Hagelin identifies numerous parallels between the qualities of the single unified field sought by Einstein and the qualities of consciousness. He argues that consciousness is the unified field.

As further proof that the unified field of consciousness and the unified field of nature are the same, Dr. Hagelin states that the qualities found at the fundamental level of nature's functioning — all possibilities, freedom, unboundedness, self-sufficiency, orderliness, bliss, and omniscience, to name a few — "are regularly experienced by people practicing Transcendental Meditation when they dive deep within and explore the more fundamental aspects of intelligence in the mind."

This unified field of consciousness that is the unified field of nature is your own inner nature as well — it is your inner *being*. It is from here that all impulses of creativity emerge. The reality of life, which was once shrouded in mysticism, is today being understood in terms of modern physics. As with all new discoveries time is needed for new concepts to be assimilated. For example, what we today consider to be one of the most obvious of ideas — that the earth is round and that it circles the Sun — when this was initially introduced, it astounded even the most advanced thinkers of that era. And it took generations of debate, pondering and persecution of its exponents before the concept was finally assimilated by the general populace.

The unified field is the field of all possibilities because it is the home of all the laws of nature. As the home of all the laws of nature we can say that this unified field is the residence of the constitution of the universe. This is the level from which all of nature manifests. And it does so according to its inherent constitution, the laws of nature that reside therein. And this unified field of the universe has now been discovered to be the unified field of consciousness. This unified field of consciousness contains within it all possibilities because all the laws of nature reside within it.

Physics has identified the unified field as the primordial essence of creation. It is *isness*, it is *being*, it is the totality of all that exists. It is existence itself. THIS UNIFIED FIELD OF CONSCIOUSNESS, THIS UNIFIED FIELD OF ALL THAT EXISTS, THIS HOME OF ALL THE LAWS OF NATURE, THIS FIELD OF ALL POSSIBILITIES, IS THE INNER DOMAIN OF THE HUMAN *BEING* — IT IS YOUR INNER DOMAIN. YOU ARE PART OF THE UNIVERSE. SO, WITHIN YOU IS THIS SAME BASIC CONSTITUENT OF LIFE; THAT UNIFIED FIELD, THE HOME OF EVERYTHING, THE FIELD OF ALL POSSIBILITIES. THIS IS YOUR BIRTHRIGHT!

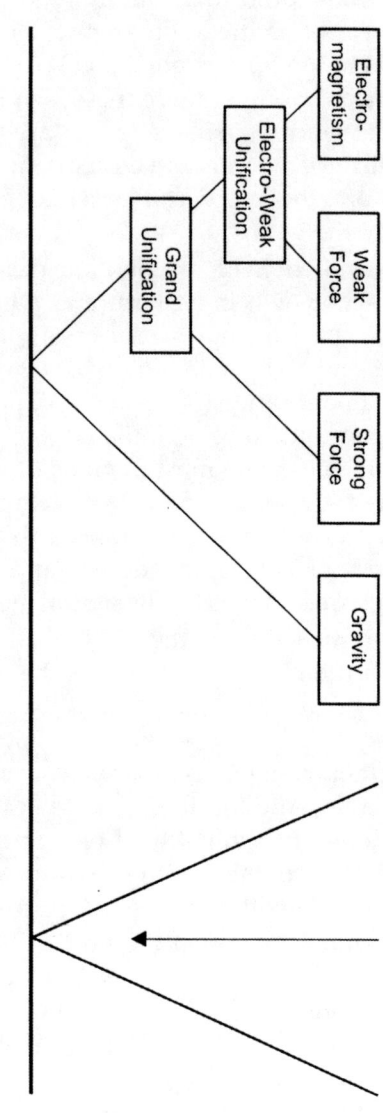

Physical Universe

Conscious Mind

Electro-magnetism	Weak Force	Strong Force	Gravity

Electro-Weak Unification

Grand Unification

Fundamental Level of Nature
Unified State of All Force and Matter Fields

Fundamental Level of Mind
Transcendental Consciousness

UNIFIED FIELD OF ALL THE LAWS OF NATURE

Fig. 2. The Unified Field identified by physics as the unified state of all the force and matter fields in nature is identical to the state of transcendental consciousness, which any individual can experience during the practice of the Transcendental Meditation technique.

References: *Modern Science and Vedic Science*, vol. 1, no. 1, 1987, pp. 29-87, and vol 3, no. 1, 1989, pp. 3-72.

Because this unified field of consciousness is your own inner nature you need not look far to find it. It is easily experienced through the practice of the TM technique. All you need to do is to bring your awareness to the deep inner level of unified consciousness, and imbibe that status within your conscious awareness. Operating from that status you gain command and support of all the laws of nature. And *all* means 'all.' This point will be developed further in Part II of this book.

The knowledge of how to contact that level deep within oneself to make use of one's inner abundant resources is the TM technique. It has been brought into the world by an Indian scholar and teacher, Maharishi Mahesh Yogi. Maharishi was revered as the most devoted and successful student of Swami Brahmananda Saraswati, a direct custodian of the wise teachings of ancient India. Now, for the first time, the essence of this ancient wisdom has been formulated into a program of study readily adaptable to the active Westerner's lifestyle.

Over five million people world-wide have started practicing the TM technique and reported almost miraculous effects on their daily lives. The interest of the scientific community was aroused. Since 1958, when the TM program was introduced to the world, over 600 scientific published studies have been conducted at over 200 universities and research institutions, including Harvard Medical School, Stanford University, University of Chicago, and UCLA. Also, many corporations have introduced the TM technique to their employees. Among them are General Motors Corporation, American Telephone and Telegraph Company, Sternberger Motor Corporation, P.A. Medical Corporation, Sunnydale Farms and Sumitomo Heavy Industries.

The following news release appeared in 1977 about TM instruction in General Motors:

> Instruction in the Transcendental Meditation technique is now eligible for full coverage under the "General Motors Corporation Tuition Assistance Plan Professional Development" component for all salaried employees in the United States.
>
> Occupational stress has been found to be the major cause of diminished health and personal productivity costing American businesses up to $200 billion annually. Over 600 comparative studies have found the TM technique to be the most effective corporate stress management program in the world today. Over the past 25 years, a number of worksite studies on the TM program have reported major benefits in all areas of employee and organizational development

and success. For example, a study of 125 General Motors employees found that their practice of the TM technique resulted in significant improvements in health, job effectiveness and satisfaction, and interpersonal relationships. The study, which was published in the journal *Anxiety, Stress and Coping*, also reported that the employees enjoyed reductions in anxiety, insomnia, fatigue, job tension, and cigarette and hard liquor use.

Results of scientific studies have repeatedly demonstrated the efficacy of the TM technique to bring fulfillment to all aspects of an individual's life. Following is an overview of some of the scientifically validated benefits:

Benefits for the Company

Improved productivity
Increased creativity
Improved job performance
Increased sales and profits
Improved teamwork and communication
Reduced stress
Improved employee health
Reduced absenteeism and sick days
Reduced need for health care
Reduced job accidents and injuries

Benefits for Executives

Increased creativity and intelligence
Broader comprehension with increased ability to focus
Improved problem-solving and decision making
Reduction of stress and tension
More energy and vitality
Reversal of biological aging
Improved relations with colleagues and employees
Improved family life
Reduced high blood pressure and cholesterol

Benefits for Employees

Improved efficiency
Increased alertness

Fewer mistakes, improved work safety
Improved job performance with less stress
Reduced job worry and tension
Reduced fatigue
Better mental and physical health
Better work relationships
Increased happiness and job satisfaction
Improved family life
Reduced smoking, alcohol consumption and drug abuse

The TM technique is holistic in scope because it enables one to make contact with that unbounded pure potentiality of life that lies deep within every individual. To my knowledge no other technique or program for self-development achieves this. Results of the scientific research studies point to the TM technique as a new paradigm in human development.

Now let's take a closer look at the mechanics of how the TM technique works so that we can better understand it as a sales training tool.

Chapter IV

The TM Technique

I first heard about the TM technique in 1968 when a newscaster announced that an introductory lecture was to be given by Maharishi Mahesh Yogi accompanied by several of his instructors at Madison Square Garden. I was always interested in mental development, so it was natural for me to investigate the claims being made about the TM technique.

My first impression was favorable. All of the instructors representing the TM organization were neatly groomed, well-dressed and businesslike, with no shaved heads, beads, chanting, or weird displays of behavior that oftentimes accompany a meditative practice. Also, I was told that there would be no need to modify my lifestyle, no special diet to follow, and no pretzel-like postures to do. "The TM technique is a simple, effortless, mental technique that rapidly unfolds one's mental potential. There is no concentration, contemplation, or some form of hypnosis involved in the practice," stated one of the panel members. This seemed strange to me because I could not conceive of a mental technique which would not require either concentration, contemplation, or some form of hypnosis. The speakers who were extolling the benefits resulting from the practice of the TM technique would give a snake oil huckster a tough act to follow. I decided to give the TM technique a try.

Now, thirty-four years later, and a qualified instructor of the TM program myself, I can personally attest to the fact that the claimed benefits of Transcendental Meditation are true. Initially, I did not understand what the TM technique was, and it was not until I began the practice, and experienced the technique working for me, that I understood what it was the instructors were so enthusiastically trying to say. Now, I am faced with the same dilemma. I need to explain an abstract concept in written words. It is actually concrete. But it is concrete only insofar as one can relate it to one's own experience. For example, how do you explain the taste of mushrooms to someone who has never tasted them? Since the TM technique is not concentration, contemplation, or some form of hypnosis, it becomes difficult to understand. All other forms of self-improvement programs fall within the categories of concentration, contemplation, or hypnosis.

Concentration exercises are tedious, difficult and often are accompanied by a feeling of fatigue or stress—some tension is felt—due to the effort that is exerted. Examples of concentration exercises are operant conditioning, gazing at candles or a spot, fixing the mind on an idea, etc. Contemplation includes, in general, the type of mental activity characterized by daydreaming, self-analysis, sensitivity sessions, and other thought-provoking type of situations. Hypnosis is of three types: self-hypnosis, you hypnotizing someone else, and someone else hypnotizing you. Included in this scheme are: pep talk motivational training, mood-making, autosuggestion, positive thinking, receiving incentives to action from subliminal sources, and programmed conditioned responses through the manipulation of the will.

In contradistinction, the TM technique is something that does its own doing. You do not do it. It works of its own nature. There is no suggestion or manipulation of mental or physical activity involved. You do not have to believe in the TM technique in order for it to work. No amount of belief aids the process. Likewise, disbelief is no hindrance to the process. In doing the TM technique you only need to create a condition and let it happen on its own. Creating a condition is the extent of the doing. This is difficult to understand because you are used to applying effort in everything that you do. To think of something that produces such great benefits, and that is simple, natural, and spontaneous, is difficult. Further, the TM technique cannot be taught, it can only be learned. And anyone who can think can learn to meditate. The TM technique can be learned by anyone over four years old, regardless of race, creed, national origin, educational level, or intellectual or emotional development.

By definition, *Transcendental Meditation* means 'to cause to go beyond thinking.' *Trans* means 'beyond,' and *scend* means 'to cause to go.' And *meditation* means 'thinking.' The TM technique enables one to transcend thought and thereby bring one's awareness to the source of thought; one's own inner self. Earlier we identified that inner self to be existence itself—*being*.

22

Thoughts are said to have energy because they flow. And thoughts have intelligence because they choose a direction. Every thought impulse, therefore, is an expression of energy and intelligence. Hence, the source of thought must be an infinite reservoir of energy and intelligence. Every human *being* is connected to this source to one extent or another. Psychologists tell us that we use only a fraction of our mental potential, which gives us a clue just how poorly most people draw on their inner resources.

The TM technique enables you to make daily contact with this omnipotent and omniscient reservoir of energy and intelligence — the inner aspect of your own nature — in a systematic way. Self-discipline is not required to do the TM technique. It is enjoyable and you will look forward to doing it. It takes only a few minutes morning and evening. It is not something that you need to do for a few months with the hope of noticing some results. The benefits begin from the first day one begins TM, and the growing benefits derived from each succeeding meditation are self-reinforcing.

How does one contact that level of life deep within one's self and make use of one's inner abundant resource? The answer is very simple. If there is a difficulty in understanding the answer it lies in the simplicity of the answer. Our own experience tells us that our mind wanders. But why does the mind wander? And is this wandering random? One statement will answer both questions — the natural tendency of the mind is to seek greater charm. The mind leaves one thing because it is no longer charming to the mind. The mind, although appearing to drift aimlessly, is seeking something more charming. We know from prior discussion that that level of life deep within us contains the full potentiality of life. If it contains the full potentiality of life it must contain maximum charm. And if it contains maximum charm the mind will naturally want to connect with it because that is the tendency of the mind; to go to a field of greater charm. All the mind needs is a means whereby it can transcend to that level of maximum charm.

To better understand the TM technique we can consider thoughts as coming from the source of thought in the same way as tiny bubbles of air would come up from the bottom of a pond. As the bubbles of air come up to the surface they become bigger and bigger, eventually popping up on the surface. Likewise, as thoughts emerge they become more and more concrete, less abstract, until they come to the surface level of the mind at which point we become aware of them as thoughts. See Fig. 3. The TM technique enables one to go from the surface thinking level of the mind to experience thought in its prior stages of development, i.e., to experience increasingly finer levels of a thought, and then to transcend the finest level of the thought to arrive at the source of thought, *being* – imbibe the nature of *being* into one's awareness, and with that awareness as a basis, perform action.

To facilitate this inward vertical stroke of the mind it is necessary to have two elements: a vehicle for the mind to use in order for it to transcend, and a technique for using the vehicle. The vehicle that is used is a particular thought. A thought has two aspects to it; it has meaning and it has a *sound* quality. Take, for example, the Spanish word *bueno*. Assuming you do not know Spanish this word will have no meaning to you, but it does have a sound. And the thought of that word is the subtle aspect of its sound. The thought that is used in the practice of the TM technique is chosen based on its "sound" suitability, i.e., its resonating quality with an individual's nervous system. There is no associated meaning to the sounds used in the TM technique. Were there an associated meaning the mind would dwell on that level of meaning, thereby remaining on the surface horizontal thinking level caught up in some mood or daydream. This would be contemplation, not transcending.

Due to the resonating quality of the vehicle used in the TM practice, the experience of the vehicle, i.e., suitable thought, at increasingly finer levels is accompanied by increasing charm. If you recall, the natural tendency of the mind is to seek increasing charm. Hence, the inward march of the mind occurs in a natural, easy, spontaneous manner. We create a condition which enables the mind to transcend, and then we allow the natural tendency of the mind to take the mind to its source. For example, if we want to go to sleep we create a condition suitable for sleep to come. We turn off the lights, lie down comfortably, close the eyes, and sleep naturally comes. To do the TM technique we sit comfortably in a chair, close the eyes, mentally use the sound as instructed, and naturally slip into the transcendental state of the unified field of pure consciousness, thereby making direct contact with that infinite reservoir of energy and intelligence – that unmanifested field of pure potentiality – deep within us. We do not lie down to do the TM technique because, from habit, we may fall asleep in that position.

Incidentally, the sounds used in the TM practice are called *mantras*. Mantras are sounds with known effects. The mantras used in the

Principle of Transcending

FIELD OF ACTION

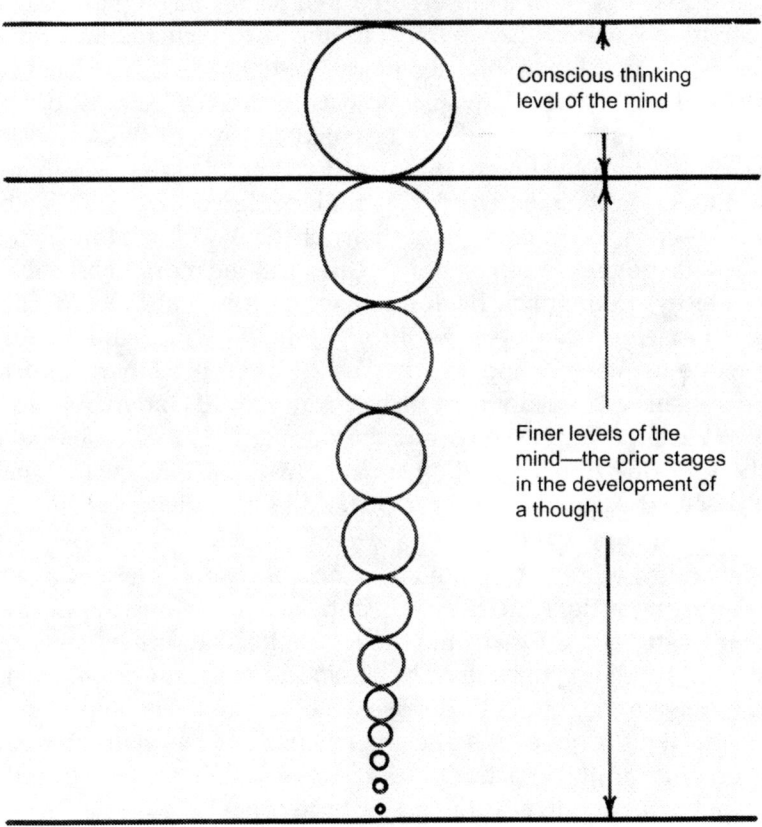

Conscious thinking
level of the mind

Finer levels of the
mind—the prior stages
in the development of
a thought

BEING

Fig. 3. The TM technique enables one's awareness to go
from the surface thinking level of the mind to experience
thought in its prior stages of development and finally to
transcend the finest thinking level to arrive at the source
of thought, *being.*

TM practice have the effect of allowing the mind to transcend. The selection of suitable mantras for individuals and the technique of experiencing the mantra at its increasingly finer levels to arrive at the source of thought is the essence of the ancient wise teachings. It is this teaching that has been a closely guarded secret throughout history. Swami Brahmananda Saraswati was the direct custodian of these secret teachings. Upon his departure, Indian scholar, teacher and monk, Maharishi Mahesh Yogi, who was revered as his most devoted and successful student, received the custodianship of this knowledge in sacred trust. According to tradition, this knowledge was only to be passed along to the next worthy custodian. However, seeing a world in chaos — crime rampant in every part of the world, continued wars, world-wide poverty, hunger and disease, and the moral fabric of society in decay — Maharishi, having the solution in hand, could not, in good conscience, deny people throughout the world the means to regenerate themselves and society. For this reason, Maharishi formulated this ancient wisdom into a program readily adaptable to the active Westerner's life style, and he specially trained some 40,000 teachers world-wide, entrusting each of them with the custodianship of this sacred science in order to make this knowledge of inner life available to people everywhere.

This knowledge, unfortunately, cannot be communicated by written description alone. It must be imparted on a one-to-one basis, teacher to student. At that time the instructor determines the appropriate mantra that is to be used by the individual, and provides guidance in the simple, but delicate, use of the mantra. The experience of transcending is a novel one and the presence of the instructor at the time of learning the practice of TM is essential to answer any questions that arise, and to ensure that the individual is doing the TM technique correctly.

Were the TM technique not available to everyone, this book would be just a philosophical dissertation on achieving success. This is not the case, however. The availability of the TM technique takes this treatise out of the realm of philosophy and brings it to the reality of a scientifically measurable personal experience. The TM technique is the key to bringing one's awareness to that source of oneself which is also the source of everything in creation. The TM technique enables one to contact that primary energy and intelligence that underlies all existence. By establishing his awareness at that primordial level the salesman cannot help but become successful. Note that success is not something that needs to be attained or acquired. You already have all the ingredients for success within you. They are latent and only need to be brought forth.

Being energetic, being intelligent, being charismatic, being efficient, being wealthy, being successful, etc., are natural expressions of *being*, i.e., existence itself. The TM technique connects you to this primordial field of *being* so that these inherent creative impulses of life find their expression spontaneously and naturally in your daily activity. This is the key to successful selling.

The TM technique, by giving a vertical dimension to the mind, enabling contact with *being*, obsoletes all forms of sales training programs in the marketplace today. The quantum difference between this approach of achieving success to that of all other methods should now be evident.

Consider the naïve gardener who is confronted with the task of curing a withering tree. He works on each withering leaf trying to modify it, wash it, clean it up, add some wire supports, paint it, etc. The experienced gardener, realizing that a tree is nourished from within, simply waters the root and enjoys the fruit. See Fig. 4. The gardener with an expanded vision knows that the solution is not found by manipulations on the level of effects. He does not treat the symptoms. It is necessary to get to the root cause of the withering condition of all of the leaves. It is obvious that nourishment from within is required. Likewise, the numerous problems of salesmen, which can be likened to the many withering leaves, are not solved on the level of the problems. Sales trainers should realize that emotional inhibitors, lack of energy, loss of enthusiasm, poor health, procrastination, lack of efficiency, etc., are all *symptoms*. The solution is not going to be found in the use of pep talks, motivational training, sensitivity sessions, contemplative mood-making, or the like, since these all deal on the level of symptoms. All of the salesmen's problems can be resolved by nourishing salesmen from deep within their own *being*. Give salesmen the method of contacting their infinite reservoir of energy and intelligence which is their own inner nature and success will be experienced in all aspects of their lives. The TM technique achieves this. It enables the salesmen to contact, and systematically draw on, the source of existence itself, and thereby make use of the full potentiality of life. This is why the TM technique is the holistic approach to sales training and development.

Fig. 4. The Holistic Approach to Sales Training

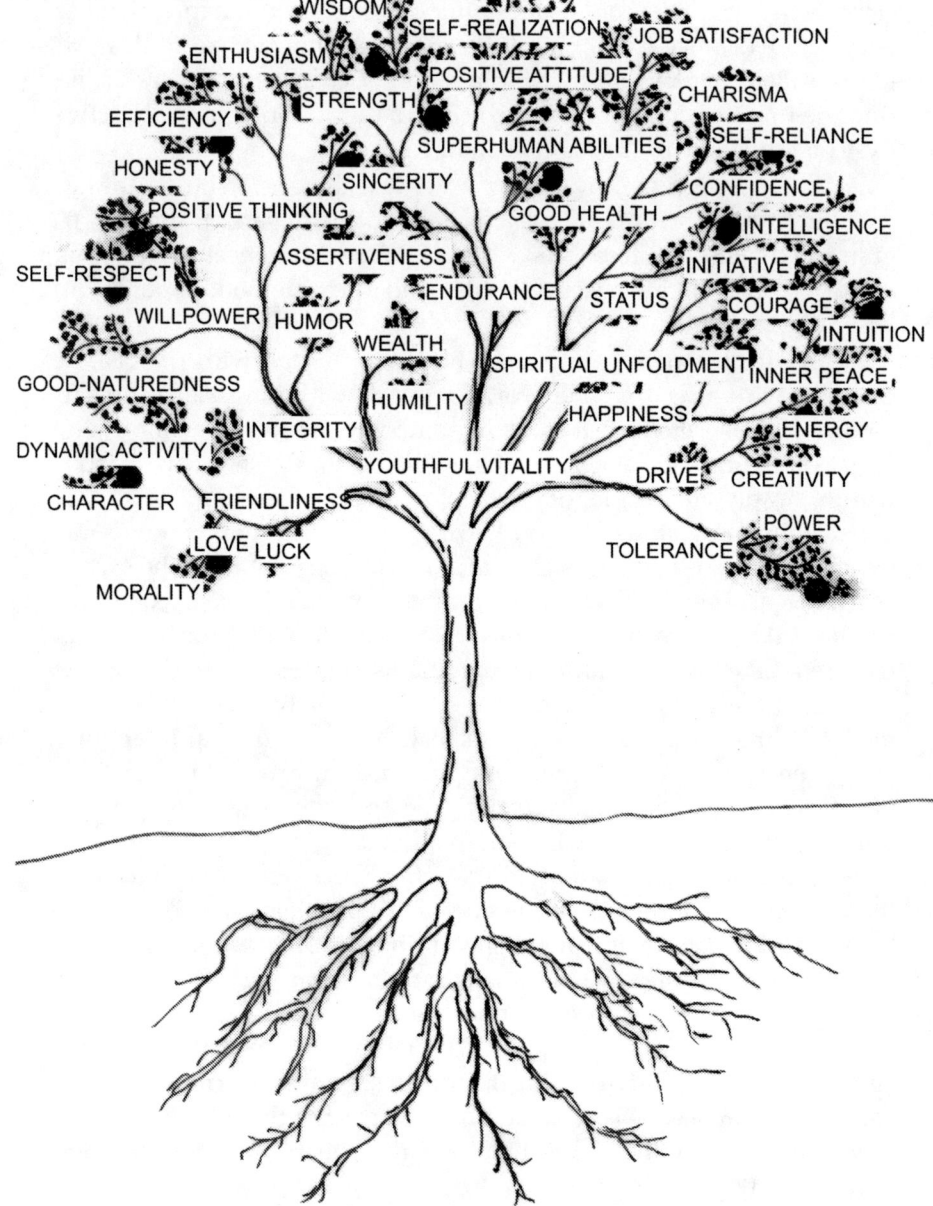

Water the root to enjoy the fruit.

Several books and numerous articles have been written about the benefits derived from the practice of the TM technique. Commenting on all of the benefits is beyond the scope of this book. I have, however, summarized a handful of the more salient benefits which will interest you as a salesman. The next several chapters highlight these benefits.

Chapter V

Gaining More Energy

One of the most important requisites for success in selling is your energy level. Drive, aggressiveness, stamina, power, motivation and enthusiasm all have energy as their basis. The higher your energy level is the more you will exhibit these attributes in your daily activity. This is natural. The natural tendency of life is to have more, to enjoy more. Life evolves toward greater fulfillment. Give a salesman more energy and he will naturally increase his productivity.

Highly successful people have noticed that when they set very high goals for themselves, they work hard to achieve those goals. Setting higher goals to achieve more may be true up to a point. But what good is it to set high goals for yourself if you do not have the energy to meet those goals? In my opinion, the goal-setting superstars are successful primarily because they have the energy to meet their goals. Successful salesmen have a high level of energy. That is why they can work hard at selling. The present school of thought, however, is to set high goals and then use a variety of pep talk, motivational-type training sessions in order to emotionally charge-up the salesman to meet those goals with nervous energy. It might get a salesman to push himself harder. But it is similar to pressing down on the accelerator of your car while in first gear. You will feel the straining of the car if you keep this process going. The same holds true for the salesman who attempts to meet his goals based on a hyped-up emotional charge from a pep talk. The strain to keep up the pace, sooner or later, catches up with him. Chronic fatigue, salesman-burnout, and sales-slump results. The less fortunate — like two associates of mine — drop dead from heart attacks. In the long haul pep talks do not substitute for lack of energy. Eventually, salesmen become desensitized to pep talks. To keep salesmen excited, sales trainers are continually contriving new gimmicks, slogans, charts, etc., with which to prod salesmen into higher productivity.

A fresh approach to motivating salesmen is necessary. We know from physics that the deeper we go into matter the more energy there is. The atomic level is more powerful than the molecular level, and the subatomic level is still more powerful than the atomic level. Mind is a subtle form of matter. We have reviewed in Chapter III that matter has its basis in consciousness. At each successively finer level of thought there is increasing power, more energy. The source of thought is the source of life itself. It is the primary energy that underlies all existence. It is an infinite reservoir of energy, and it is the same field of pure potentiality that lies deep within you. This is your inner self which we discussed earlier.

The TM technique, by giving the mind the opportunity to experience thought at increasingly finer levels, and ultimately to transcend the finest level of thinking, directly connects you to the powerhouse. During the practice of Transcendental Meditation the body and mind draw from this inner reservoir of energy. A few minutes of charging your batteries via TM in the A.M. is sufficient to enable a full day of vigorous activity. Then, another short period of recharging before dinner provides more energy for continued dynamic activity throughout the evening.

A salesman with more energy automatically sets higher goals for himself. He becomes self-motivated. Self-motivation is really motivation from the level of one's own inner nature—the *self*. Productivity automatically increases. And when a salesman is able to meet his goals, job satisfaction increases proportionately. Pilot studies at General Motors Corporation and American Telephone and Telegraph Company support the findings of Dr. David R. Frew; persons practicing the TM technique show increased productivity, more job satisfaction, and less desire to change jobs.

Procrastination is caused primarily by lack of energy. When fatigue sets in, the mind contrives a variety of excuses to delay action in order to give the system badly needed rest. It is natural to procrastinate when you run out of energy. This is the body's built-in safeguard. You do not eliminate procrastination by pep talks. More energy automatically minimizes procrastination. I say "minimizes" because three other factors fuel procrastination: emotional inhibitors; bad health; and a weak mind. These factors are dealt with in later chapters.

How often have you felt that you did not have enough time? Is it really the lack of time that cheats you from success? Then what accounts for the tremendous success some salesmen have who possess the same twenty-four hours per day? Do they have more intelligence, more efficiency? Maybe, to an extent. But their energy plays the more important role.

The TM technique does not only connect you to your inner powerhouse, but, by virtue of making that connection, also rejuvenates the entire nervous system. The TM technique gives you "bounce-back" and endurance.

We know from psychology that the mind and body are interrelated. As you influence the mind so you produce an effect within the body, and vice versa. During the TM practice, as one experiences thoughts at increasingly finer levels, mental activity becomes less and less. As a result, physical activity becomes less. The body gains a very deep profound rest, much deeper than deep sleep.

Dr. Robert Keith Wallace, who did pioneer research studies at UCLA and Harvard Medical School on the physiological effects of practicing the TM technique, was the first scientist to identify a fourth major state of consciousness, unlike waking, dreaming or sleeping. His research was published in *Science* and *Scientific American*. Oxygen consumption, heart rate, skin resistance, electroencephalograph (EEG) measurements, and blood lactate were recorded prior, during and after subjects practiced the TM technique. What was found was that a unique physiological state occurred which was unlike the waking, sleeping or dreaming states of consciousness. The body entered into a very deep, profound state of rest. Yet, the EEG recording disclosed a wakeful condition characterized by marked intensification of alpha waves. See Fig. 5.

The novelty of these findings and those of subsequent studies conducted by other researchers has given rise to the hypothesis that a fourth major state of consciousness had been discovered.

Comparative physiological studies were made on hypnotized subjects and no correlation was found between the hypnotic state and the state achieved by the practice of the TM technique. Hypnosis produced no significant change in the metabolic index. In hypnosis the physiology of the subject took on the form characteristic of the mental state which had been suggested to the subject. Likewise, this study reported that there was no comparison to the state achieved in the TM practice to those states that can be achieved by operant conditioning, such as alpha-feedback training. See Fig. 6.

The TM State Compared to Other States of Consciousness

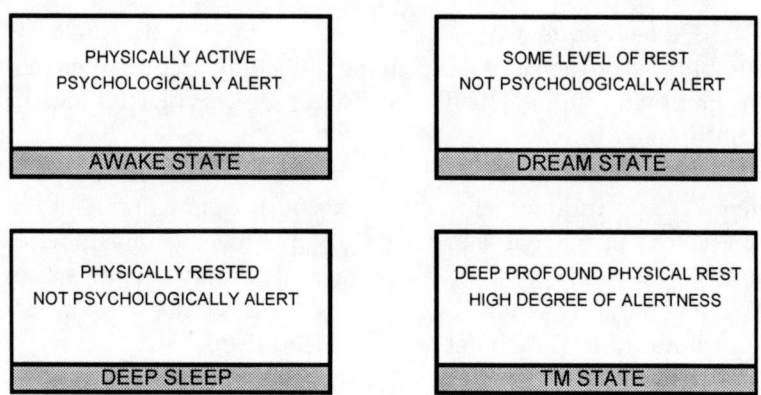

PHYSICALLY ACTIVE PSYCHOLOGICALLY ALERT	SOME LEVEL OF REST NOT PSYCHOLOGICALLY ALERT
AWAKE STATE	DREAM STATE
PHYSICALLY RESTED NOT PSYCHOLOGICALLY ALERT	DEEP PROFOUND PHYSICAL REST HIGH DEGREE OF ALERTNESS
DEEP SLEEP	TM STATE

Fig. 5. Unlike the Waking, Dreaming and Deep Sleep states of consciousness, the Transcendental State (TM State) of consciousness is characterized by deep rest coincident with a high level of alertness.

The TM technique is the basis for increased dynamic activity. An archer draws his arrow back—in the opposite direction—a little bit, and then lets go. The arrow flies far. It is a simple technique which gives the dynamic thrust to the arrow. Likewise, the TM technique draws the mind back, to its source. This brings the entire system into contact with the powerhouse. Simultaneously, due to the profound state of rest that is achieved, the salesman is revitalized. This prepares the salesman for a day of dynamic activity. Further, because a day's work is met with a greater resource of energy, less fatigue occurs. Individuals practicing the TM technique report a need to sleep less.

Fred Gratzon, CEO, Telegroup, Inc., a long-distance discount carrier and one of the fastest growing companies in America, states:

> More than half our work force practices the Transcendental Meditation program, and the effect has been simply astounding. We are more efficient, productive and profitable than ever. The atmosphere in the office is much calmer than in other companies, yet the air bristles with creativity and dynamism. I credit this program with the rapid success of our company, and recommend it to everyone else in business.

Levels of Rest—Change in Metabolic Rate

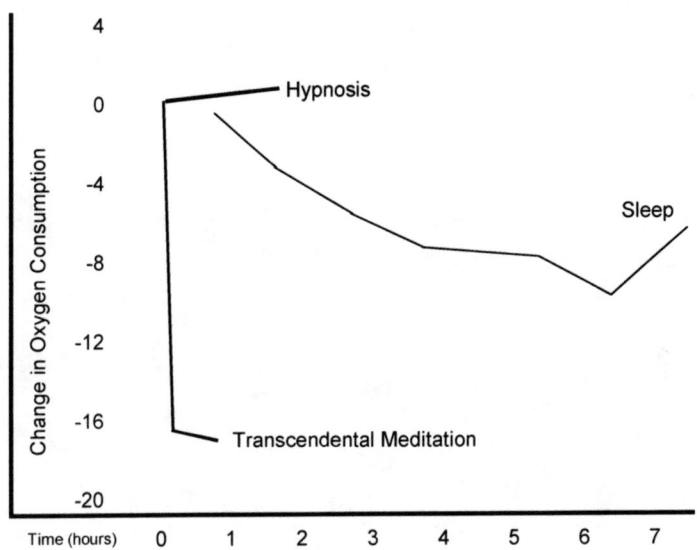

Fig. 6. During Transcendental Meditation oxygen consumption and metabolic rate markedly decrease, indicating a deep state of rest, even deeper than that achieved during sleep. Hypnosis produced no significant change in the metabolic rate.

Reference: *Scientific American*, February, 1972.

These benefits resulting from the practice of the TM technique have applications in many fields. General Franklin M. Davis-Retired, who presided over the U.S. Army war college, has become an outspoken advocate of the TM technique as a means to strengthen the armed forces. As a result, the TM program has been made available at military bases across the United States. Also, major airlines have implemented pilot programs and are finding that TM eliminates fatigue and neutralizes jetlag — something for the traveling salesman to consider. Joe Namath, Larry Bowa, Willie Stargell, Steve Carlton and Bill Walton — to name a few athletes — have used the TM technique to give them the edge in fierce competition. The TM technique gives the salesman the edge in the fierce competition of selling. The TM technique is done for the sake of dynamic activity.

So for sales' sake meditate!

Chapter VI

Unfolding Your Mental Potential

Whatever you desire in life you can achieve. You probably agree with this statement, at least in principle. If you are a student of the positive thinking school of thought you have to believe that you can achieve your desires. But how many salesmen who honestly believe that they can achieve their desires are living fulfilled lives? Is belief in this philosophical principle sufficient for achieving success? No. Something more is necessary. What is needed is the *means* to achieve the fulfillment of desires.

In order to achieve we must first act. And we have already seen that action is based on thinking, and thinking has its basis in the source of thought. It is only necessary to use more of your mental potential in order to gain more fulfillment in activity. Tap the source of thought, make full use of your potential, and enjoy total fulfillment of desires. Successful people are people who use more of their mental potential.

Psychologists say that we use only about 10% of our mental potential. There is, however, a paradox in that statement. How can someone who is using less than his full mental potential know what is the totality of the mind and be able to claim that man uses only 10% of that totality? There may be dimensions to the mind far beyond that which our narrow vision is capable of comprehending. Those individuals who have unfolded their mental potential say that the average man uses only about one-millionth of his mental potential, and that might be an understatement.

Mind is the greatest natural resource and the ultimate power. In its unmanifested, absolute state it is pure consciousness, pure intelligence, pure potentiality. It is that basic field of intelligence which permeates and gives order to all forms of relative existence, that is, all aspects of activity. That source of intelligence is the source of life itself. This source, we have seen, can be understood in terms of the absolute, unified field in quantum physics, which has inherent within it all qualities of the relative state, but in an unmanifested form. The unified field is the state of least excitation. It is characterized by perfect orderliness wherein all the laws of nature and all possibilities of manifestation exist. This state, therefore, is omniscient. The omniscient source of intelligence is that which gives direction and harmony to the entire field of creation from the galaxies to the subatomic particles, and this is the same source of intelligence which gives rise to our thoughts and actions.

The TM technique opens our awareness to this basic value of life deep within us. The TM technique connects us to this source, which is our inner self. During the practice of the TM technique the mind takes an inward, vertical dive within itself by experiencing thought at increasingly finer stages, finally to connect with the source of thought. Then, returning from that state the conscious mind grows in the nature of the inner value of life. By repeatedly bringing the mind back and forth between the conscious thinking level and the finer stages in the development of a thought, the finer levels of the mind become increasingly familiar to the conscious thinking level. An expansion of awareness occurs. Ultimately, this expansion encompasses the full breadth of the mind; one's conscious thinking becomes established in the source of thought itself. The finer, more powerful levels of the mind, heretofore hidden from use, become part of our *normal* daily conscious awareness and use. See Fig. 7. As a result, thinking becomes more powerful, more orderly and more creative. Learning ability increases. A salesman whose mind is more powerful and orderly will find his speech and actions more powerful and orderly. He will naturally assume and maintain control of the selling scenario. He will have will power and a one-pointedness of purpose.

A salesman with expanded and orderly thinking is able to understand relationships and come to creative solutions. And a salesman with increased learning ability can digest the continual flood of technical product data, corporate memos, sales tips, competitive market reports, data on business trends, etc., so essential to his livelihood. Salesmen who practice the TM technique do not become obsolete due to the exponential growth of technology that is occurring today. A salesman whose mental capacity has been expanded can learn more easily and can retain more. Learning is not a task or a strain for some-

Unfoldment of Mental Potential Through the TM Technique

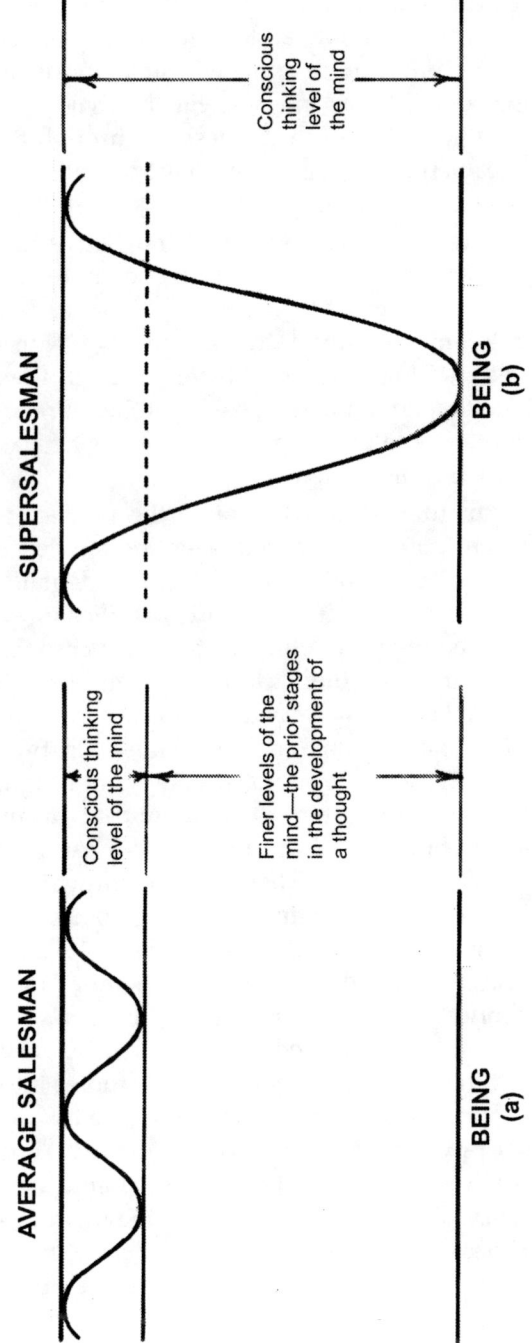

Fig. 7. By practicing the TM technique the surface conscious thinking level of an average salesman (a) expands to encompass the full range of the mind, a supersalesman status (b).

one who has increased capacity to learn. With an increased capacity for gaining knowledge one naturally wants to learn more. Reading speed, comprehension, concentration and memory spontaneously improve. The salesman becomes more knowledgeable and is able to converse in a wide range of fields and interests. Further, sales trainers, by increasing the learning capacity of their salesmen through the TM technique, can train salesmen better in a wider range of skills, thereby reducing the need for "team sales calls."

Transcendental Meditation instructors say, "Knowledge is structured in consciousness." Knowledge is a direct function of expanding awareness. As consciousness expands learning increases. Modern psychology states that learning ability decreases with age. Nonsense! The TM technique makes that statement obsolete. Through the practice of the TM technique the older a person becomes the more knowledge he gains. Therefore, as a salesman matures in years he becomes more valuable to himself and his company.

The unfoldment of mental potential through the practice of the TM technique is not conjecture. Controlled scientific studies prove that the benefits claimed by the proponents of Transcendental Meditation are not merely subjective speculations. EEG studies on practitioners of the TM technique revealed a high order of synchronization in alpha brain wave activity from the back to the front of the brain. Occasionally, periods of beta brain wave activity occurred which were also synchronized and in phase from all points on the scalp. Synchronization of brain wave activity was also noted between the right and left cerebral hemispheres. It is important to point out that this unique condition of orderliness in brain physiology results as a natural effect from the practice of the TM technique. There is no attempt at operant conditioning or special training. These findings were reported in *Electroencephalography and Clinical Neurophysiology*," Vol. 33, 1972, and in Vol. 35, 1973. The studies were conducted by Dr. Jean-Paul Banquet at Stanley Cobb Laboratories for Psychiatric Research, Massachusetts General Hospital, and at Harvard Medical School. Researchers at MERU, a Swiss research institution, doing advanced studies into consciousness, and identifying parallels between consciousness and the principles of physics, draw a correlation between the orderliness of the brain caused by the practice of the TM technique and the Third Law of Thermodynamics. The Third Law of Thermodynamics states that maximum orderliness is achieved when the temperature (activity) of a given system is decreased. Of course, during the practice of the TM technique we are not reducing the temperature of our brains. However, we are reducing mental activity. With the reduction in mental activity orderliness in the functioning of the brain occurs. This makes sense since the source of thought is that least excited state of the mind which contains all the laws of nature in unmanifested form. Experience tells us that this unmanifested field of pure potentiality must be orderly since all of creation which springs forth from this source is orderly. The TM technique brings our awareness to this level of orderliness and structures that orderliness on the level of our thinking. A mind structured in orderliness must produce orderly and powerful thinking, speech and action.

Positive thinking aims the mind in the right direction. But it is powerful thinking that enables you to achieve that at which you aim. The difference between positive thinking and powerful thinking is like aiming a flashlight at the moon compared to aiming a laser light at the moon. A strong, powerful mind gives the salesman the wherewithal to do what he wants to do. A powerful mind, therefore, helps counter procrastination.

The average person's brain waves are scattered, diffused, much like the light from an ordinary light bulb. The brain waves of practitioners of the TM technique are synchronized and may be compared to the synchrony found in a laser light. The difference between the light from a light bulb versus a laser light is the synchronization of wave activity. Likewise, the difference between the average salesman and the supersalesman is brain-wave synchrony. It is brain-wave synchrony that gives concentrated power to thought and enables one to perform superhuman abilities such as to levitate one's body by mere intention—more about that later.

Gary Bogart of McCandless, national sales manager for WPXI-TV, Pittsburgh, has been practicing the TM technique for more than three years. He explains, "I was trying to find a way to ease stress, and TM also helps you focus more."

Steven Rubin, Chairman and CEO of United Fuels International, Inc. (international energy brokerage firm), states:

> For me the experience of settled inner wakefulness and expanded awareness during the Transcendental Meditation technique is the real foundation for successful decision making. After meditating I have the mental clarity and alertness for laser-like focus on the details and; at the same time, for broad comprehension so I don't get lost in the details. I find myself continuously growing in insight and

intuition, as well as in the ability to focus and analyze. Over my years in business, the TM technique has been a real competitive advantage.

Burton A. Dole, Jr., former Chairman and CEO, Puritan-Bennett Corp. (leading manufacturer of respiratory products), shares a similar view:

> The key to success in today's world is innovation, creativity — beyond anything else. If you create products and services that are clearly better than what your competitors produce, you're going to succeed in today's world. Having the ability to enhance one's own creativity as well as that of one's employees seems to me to be the ultimate responsibility of a manager within a company. And the Transcendental Meditation program allows that creativity enhancement to take place beyond anything I've ever seen.

Researchers support the anecdotal claims of meditators; they find that there is a high degree of correlation between creativity and orderly brain wave activity. Also, studies comparing TM meditators and control groups of nonmeditators show that those practicing TM exhibit increased intelligence growth rate, increased learning ability and improved memory. Research studies have also indicated that practitioners of the TM technique are more resourceful, adaptable and flexible. All these benefits are fundamental to progress. See Fig. 8 and Fig. 9.

Above all, the TM technique, by unfolding the salesman's awareness to his own inner *self*, gives the salesman knowledge of his own reality and his relationship with the universe.

Tom Gould, Chairman and CEO, Younkers, Inc. (a Midwest chain of 53 fashion department stores), states:

> My practice of the Transcendental Meditation technique has given me a 360-degree awareness. In business, I have always been very fixed and focused on my goals. Now, with the expanded awareness gained from the Transcendental Meditation program, I am able to be more open and flexible in my approaches to achieving these goals. In my personal life, I feel that I am a far more integrated, fulfilled human being.

For sales' sake meditate!

Development of Intelligence—Increased IQ

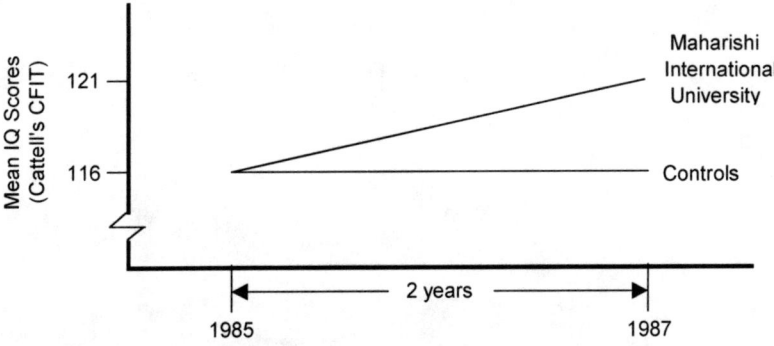

Fig. 8. Students at Maharishi University of Management (formerly Maharishi International University) in Fairfield, Iowa, who practiced the Transcendental Meditation and TM-Sidhi programs over a two-year period, showed significant increases in intelligence and mental alertness compared to a control group from another Iowa university. This study supports other research showing increased IQ and faster choice reaction by Transcendental Meditation meditators.

References: 1. *Personality and Individual Differences,* vol. 12, 1991, pp. 1105-1116.
2. *Perceptual and Motor Skills*, vol. 62, 1986, pp. 731-738.
3. *College Student Journal*, vol. 15, 1981, pp. 140-146.
4. *The Journal of Creative Behavior*, vol. 19, 1985, pp. 270-275.
5. *Journal of Clinical Psychology*, vol 42, 1986, pp.161-164.
6. *Gedrag Tijdschrift voor Psychologie* [Behavior: Journal of Psychology], vol. 3, 1975, pp. 167-182.

Iowa Tests of Basic Skills

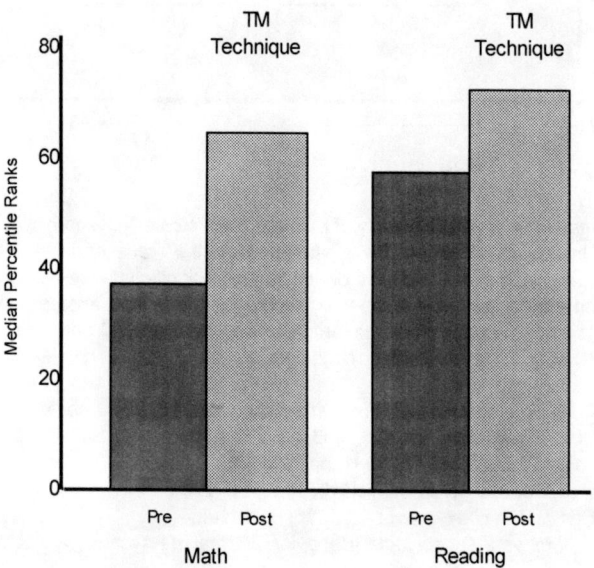

Fig. 9. After practicing the Transcendental Meditation technique for one year, school students showed significant gains on the Iowa Tests of educational development, a nationally standardized test. The relationship between months of continued practice of Transcendental Meditation and improved academic performance shows that TM directly improves the ability to learn.

References: 1. *Education*, vol 107, 1986, pp. 49-54.
2. *Education*, vol. 109, 1989, pp. 302-304.
3. *Modern Science and Vedic Science*, vol. 1, 1987, pp. 433-468.

Chapter VII

Being More Efficient

Do you have a minute? We all have come into this life with somewhere in the neighborhood of 30 to 50 million minutes, give or take a few million minutes depending upon our contract with the Creator. That is a lot of time. Yet, how often have you said to yourself that you did not have the time to do something, "If I only had the time to …?" What accounts for some individuals' staggering achievements while other individuals cannot even provide for their own basic survival needs? It is never a question of having sufficient time. It is a matter of having sufficient energy and the intelligence to know what to do with the energy you have. Look at the tremendous accomplishments of the Almighty Creator, expressing its infinite energy and intelligence to produce and sustain all the diversity of relative existence.

Man was born in the image of the Creator. We have inherent within us, as our inner divine nature, that same source of infinite energy and intelligence as that of the Creator. Man, not having his awareness established in that source, makes mistakes and then proclaims, "To err is human." This is just an excuse for not knowing how to draw from that infinite reservoir of energy and intelligence deep within us. It is an excuse for one's ignorance of the basic natural law that needs to be followed to achieve success.

Everything in nature works with harmonious, split-second precision. Only man, who has been endowed with free will, is found stumbling around, creating disharmony and experiencing failures. There is a divine plan in nature, and nature intends for everything to operate in tune with this plan. When something goes out of balance nature moves to correct the discordant note like a conductor who keeps the entire orchestra operating in harmony. In nature, like in an orchestra, there is plenty of latitude for individual expression. However, that individual expression must harmonize with the plan of the divine orchestra. Harmony is basic to nature.

45

Nature's built-in safeguard which assures that harmony is maintained is the law of cause and effect. We have all been told, "As you do unto others so it shall be done unto you." More colloquially, "What goes around comes around." Sir Isaac Newton discovered this principle in nature and stated, "For every action there is an equal and opposite reaction." A harmonious life-supporting action will produce a harmonious effect.

It should be obvious, then, that selling a bad product, that is, selling a product that is not serving one's fellow man in some positive way, cannot produce continued success. Or using sales methods and techniques that tend to deceive, manipulate or otherwise take advantage of the prospects to whom we are selling will also fail to produce continued results. That which is life-supporting, that which has a positive influence on others and the environment, will succeed. And it will succeed to the extent to which it is life-supporting. That is the basic law of cause and effect. Whatever you put into causation you effect. You can view this principle from the perspective of making a single sales call. Or you can take a broader view and consider the effects that must result from the cumulative actions of many individuals.

I recall a well-known financial analyst who published a newsletter of investment recommendations to a select group of insiders. After the insiders had the opportunity to take their investment positions, the analyst recommended the same investment to the general public via his nationally syndicated newspaper column, fully knowing that this touting would drive up the price of the investment. Then, he and his insiders would bail out making a handsome profit. He made a lot of money for himself and the insiders. At the same time, he generated a lot of ill will among the general public who were left holding the bag. I do not want to be in this analyst's shoes when "what goes around comes around."

Here is another example of how some salesmen play the game of life. A former boss of mine told me that he would show me how to close the big deals. At a meeting with the prospect my boss simply stated, "Mr. X, which would you prefer to have: $3,000 cash, or a home entertainment system delivered to your house?" as he abruptly flicked the contract over to the prospect for signing. He made the sale. But in the process he lost a good employee.

Also, there are many companies that knowingly pollute the environment and rape the earth of its natural resources with total disregard for the consequences of their actions. The basic laws of nature will not stand for man's folly. That which disturbs the harmony of nature cannot continue to survive. Our planet is a living system which requires order and balance just like an individual. Like an individual, when the planet gets sick it develops boils (volcanoes erupt); its skin cracks (earthquakes occur); it coughs, sneezes, and sweats (high winds, rains and floods prevail). Our observations of the economic situation with its many product failures and business failures and personal bankruptcies tells us that something is wrong. These are all symptomatic of a basic failure—the collective failure of people to think, speak and act in accordance with the laws of nature.

I am not attempting to make converts, preach the gospel, or expound religious doctrine. I am explaining the natural scientific law for achieving success.

Physics tells us that everything in the universe is constantly influencing everything else. Nothing exists in isolation. All thought, speech and action produces influences which affect our surroundings. How can man, then, with his limited perspective be able to analyze the consequences of every one of his thoughts, words and actions? It is not possible to determine a successful course of action on the basis of evaluating the implications of all possible thoughts, words and actions in every circumstance and problem. The scope of activity is too complex to be conquered on the basis of such an analysis. But isn't this what most sales training programs advocate?

When I was attending stockbroker sales training classes we had to memorize a flow chart of programmed responses designed to manipulate the client into a sale. We also were given a dozen, or so, canned statements to make to a client to explain our way out of any bad investment recommendations we made. Then, there were the sales tips of remembering when to accent the voice, when to nod or show facial expressions, remembering to make eye contact, showing interest in the client, asking the right questions and effectively listening to responses. At the same time, on another track of the mind, we were to read body language, and just about mentally administer the Minnesota Multiphasic Personality Inventory to determine what motivated the buyer and how to sell him. Oh, and we had to make sure not to forget to appear sincere and enthusiastic while retaining a residual recollection of how terrific we were.

This is acting school, not sales training! An actor can memorize lines and actions because he functions in a highly structured and controlled set of circumstances, and has the option to reenact a scene. A salesman functions in a highly fluid situation and needs flexibility to think, speak and act spontaneously in response to any encountered set of circumstances. When thought, speech and action are correct for a particular set of circumstances, success results.

To have correct thoughts, speech and actions it is necessary to bring our awareness to the home of all the laws of nature. The home of all the laws of nature, we have seen, is the unmanifested field of pure potentiality and perfect orderliness from where all the laws of nature function. The TM technique enables us to bring our awareness to this state of perfect orderliness. When this state gets stabilized in our conscious awareness, then spontaneously we will think, speak and act in harmony with all the laws of nature. Being in harmony with nature is the key to performing efficiently. Harmony means efficiency. When man acts in discordance with nature, resistance is created and this slows his progress. Total harmony with nature produces maximum efficiency.

Why is it that given any set of circumstances, be it a bad economy, irate boss, change in sales territory, increased competition, lack of sales leads, lack of home office support, work stoppages, delivery problems, or whatever, the top salesmen always are in the right place at the right time and land the sales? Why do sales seem to happen automatically for them and do so on a continuous basis? The answer is, they are efficient. Efficiency means right action. It means harmony. It is called luck by losers. Successful salesmen are salesmen who are more in harmony with their inner nature; they are more in tune with their inner self. Thereby, they make their own luck. As one poet put it:

> One ship sails east and another sails west
>   With the self-same winds that blow.
> 'Tis the set of the sail and not the gale
>   Which determines the way they go.
>
> As the winds of the sea are the ways of fate
>   As we voyage along through life,
> 'Tis the act of the soul that determines the goal,
>   And not the calm or the strife.

The same vast myriad of changing circumstances and possibilities are there for everyone. It is how you position yourself within these changes that determines the way you will go. The TM technique enables you to establish your awareness in harmony with the home of all the laws of nature. Your actions, therefore, will be in accordance with all the laws of nature. As a result, you must achieve success whether you believe you will or not. It is simply a matter of establishing your conscious awareness at the level of your own inner *being* and spontaneously acting from that level. This is the wise ancient teaching for achieving success.

Some salesmen achieve success through hard work alone. By pushing themselves extra hard they can overcompensate for their lack of inner-connectivity. They then proclaim that success is achieved through hard work. Work is experienced as being hard when it is not being done easily and harmoniously; when it is being forced. Work that is performed efficiently is not fatiguing. Efficiency is harmony. Establish your awareness at the level of the mind where perfect orderliness is found and your actions will be harmonious. This is the technique for efficiency.

Techniques enable us to accomplish more with less effort. If we want to move a large boulder we use the technique of a lever and with little effort we accomplish a lot. A child futilely tries to catch a floating feather by grasping at it. The air currents caused by her hand motions push the feather away from her. An adult, having a broader perspective of the laws of nature, knows to gently place an open palm beneath the falling feather which alights into the grasp with minimal effort to secure it.

The TM technique, by bringing order and efficiency to the salesman's actions, enables the salesman to accomplish much, much more for his efforts.

Success is its own positive feedback. Success results in job satisfaction. A successful salesman is optimistic and enthusiastic regardless of the radical changes in the economy and environment that may be taking place around him. The salesman whose awareness is established in the home of all the laws of nature will always come out on top regardless of external factors. What appears to be confusion and chaos in the environment to a person with a myopic vision is a harmonious display of rapid change to a person with expanded vision. The more rapid the change, the greater is the opportunity. A person whose awareness is established at the source and cause of change will act in harmony with the changes and will view even radical changes and circumstances as opportunities. He will succeed easily while others work hard and fail. It is only a matter of anchoring the mind at its

Enhanced Job Performance
and Job Satisfaction

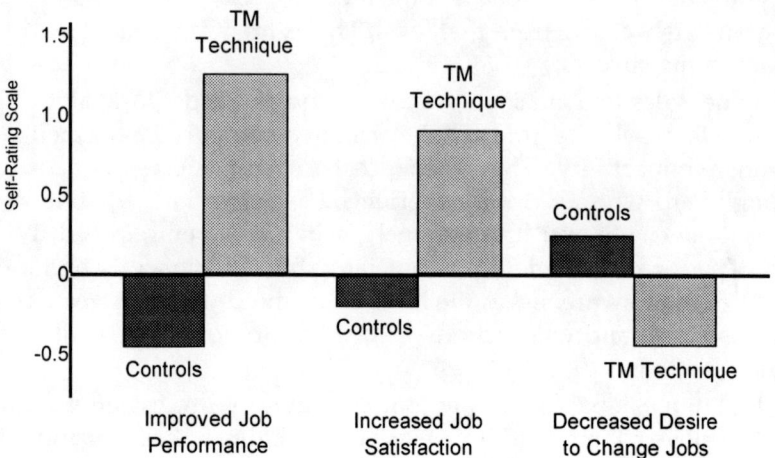

Fig. 10. Employees practicing the Transcendental Meditation technique an average of 11 months showed significant improvements at work compared to subjects of a control group; Transcendental Meditation practitioners reported improved job performance, increased job satisfaction and a decrease in desire to change jobs.

References: 1. *Academy of Management Journal*, vol 17, 1974, pp. 362-368.
2. *Scientific Research on the Transcendental Meditation Program: Collected Papers*, vol 1, 1977, pp. 630-638.
3. *Anxiety, Stress, and Coping: An International Journal*, vol. 6, 1993, pp. 245-262.

source where perfect orderliness exists, and spontaneously thinking, speaking and action will be in harmony with nature, and man will succeed because nature always succeeds.

To recap: The key to performing efficient, successful action is having an awareness established at the level of one's own inner *being*. The TM technique does this.

You will not have to practice the TM technique for weeks, months or years on the basis of faith and hope that someday you will achieve some results. No. The first inward stroke of the TM technique will connect you to your own inner *being* and this will be a quantum leap in unfolding your awareness. It is the experience of millions of people all over the world who started the TM program that results are immediate and are cumulative with the continuation of the practice.

For sales' sake meditate!

Chapter VIII

Good Health Brings Wealth

Maximum success in selling can only be achieved when the salesman has an active, vital, healthy body with a balanced mind and stable emotions. A salesman who is experiencing anxiety, tenseness, fatigue, insomnia, a migraine headache, an allergy, or any number of similar types of ailments so prevalent in the pressure cooker business and political climate of today, is going to be selling with a handicap.

I was doing some public relations work for my employer, by visiting with a data processing supervisor of one of our larger accounts. During our conversation the supervisor commented, "Do not send that fat man around. I can't stand him." I thought, "What a thing to say!" I personally liked Ted. The supervisor, perhaps had a prejudice against fat. What would you do in a situation like that? Keep sending Ted to call on the supervisor for follow-up sales and service? Ted was eventually dismissed from the company. Maybe there was more to it than just his over-weight appearance. Ted was not very graceful climbing stairs and would get short-winded quickly while trying to keep up with others. He was selling with a handicap that was robbing him of his livelihood. How many "Teds" are out there working against themselves?

The following two incidents had more severe consequences for two of my associates' sales careers. David was a hard working insurance salesman who told me he became his company's top salesman as a result of hard work. "I drive myself. I push, push and keep pushing. I have to admit that it is an obsession with me," he said. He told me that he was a workhorse and could not rid himself of competitive thoughts. He lacked balance and a broader perspective in life. Worst of all, at the height of his career, he lost life itself. "Death took the life

of David ... yesterday due to excessive stress and cardiac insuffi-
ciency," was the news report.

The second incident occurred two years later. I had just taken a
vicious and uncalled-for browbeating from my boss who periodically
lost control of himself, only later to return and apologize. The pressures of the job were too much for him to handle and he projected his
feelings of inadequacy onto others. After this last blowup, to which I
responded with total equanimity and control, my friend Marty came
to me and asked, "How can you take the beating you take under Phil
and still show no sign of wear?" Marty noticed I had something going
for me and wanted in on it. Unfortunately, before I could clue him in
he dropped dead from a heart attack. He was only 56 years old. He
often spoke of his dream to someday develop his property in Oregon
into a luxury golf course. The closest Marty came to realize his dream
was to die while teeing off at the ninth hole at his favorite golf course.

These incidents are true. I am not using poetic license to make a
point. I do not have to. I have many case histories from which to
choose. The business world is packed with people like David, Phil
and Marty who are straining at the bit to be first in the game of life.
Not knowing how to play the game of life they sacrifice their health
and, too often, their lives for achieving one small aspect of the spec-
trum of success.

I am sure that you will agree that success is not just money, or
power, or recognition for being first. Success is holistic and includes
having good physical health, peace of mind, and controlled emotions.
Health should never be compromised for acquisition of material gain.
Poor health takes the salesman's attention away from selling and, in
extreme cases, takes the salesman out of selling. In contradistinction,
good health enables the salesman to sell more, earn more and to have
more of the material comforts of life he desires.

The TM technique, by providing the salesman with improved
physical, psychological and emotional health, has a direct correlation
to the selling success of the salesman. Numerous research studies
have been performed on many persons around the world to evaluate
the effectiveness of Transcendental Meditation in the revitalization,
rejuvenation and maintenance of mental, emotional and physical
health. The following abridged list of benefits was gleaned from five
volumes entitled, *Scientific Research on the Transcendental Meditation
Program, Collected Papers*, Volumes I to V, published by MERU Press.
The Transcendental Meditation program was found to:

1. Decrease the workload and wear on the heart.
2. Gradually bring about a permanent and beneficial reduction in heart rate.
3. Reduce systolic and arterial blood pressure.
4. Improve tolerance to exercise by persons with angina pectoris.
5. Markedly decrease the concentration of blood lactate (lactate concentration in blood is directly associated with anxiety neurosis, anxiety attacks and high blood pressure).
6. Reduce and eliminate migraine headaches.
7. Reduce anxiety.
8. Reduce use of alcohol and cigarettes.
9. Increase internal control and tolerance in frustrating situations.
10. Reduce depression.
11. Reduce psychosomatic disease.
12. Strengthen the body's immune system.
13. Decrease allergies.
14. Decrease inflammation of the gums, providing a stronger basis for dental health.
15. Be a therapy for insomnia.
16. Normalize weight.
17. Reduce neuroticism.
18. Develop moral maturity.
19. Increase liveliness, friendliness and adventurousness.
20. Reduce use of nonprescribed drugs.
21. Decrease airway resistance in asthmatic patients.
22. Provide faster recovery from sleep deprivation.
23. Increase self-confidence and assertiveness.
24. Increase self-acceptance and contentment.
25. Develop a positive tendency to see man as essentially good.
26. Increase self-actualization.
27. Enable a faster pace of progress.
28. Increase spontaneity and self-sufficiency.
29. Increase endurance.
30. Decrease inhibition.
31. Increase sense of humor.
32. Increase creativity.
33. Improve thought-action coordination.
34. Speed up reaction time.
35. Improve efficiency in perception and performance.

36. Increase alertness while reducing dullness.
37. Increase perceptual ability.
38. Increase vitality.

This list is exemplary of the diverse and broad scope of benefits in the field of health resulting from the practice of the TM technique.

Results of a new study recently published in the American Heart Association's journal, *Hypertension*, indicate the TM technique was effective in lowering high blood pressure.

To date, over 6,000 physicians have learned the TM technique in the United States, and many prescribe it to their patients. Gary Kapland, MD Clinical Director of Neurophysiology, North Shore University Hospital, New York University School of Medicine states:

> Stroke is the third leading cause of death in this country. Because the leading risk factor of stroke is hypertension and because the TM technique has been shown to reduce hypertension and is free of the side effects often seen with hypertension medication, I wholeheartedly recommend the TM program to patients who have had a stroke or are at risk for a stroke.

Additionally, on file with the TM movement, are literally thousands of pages of anecdotal evidence attesting to the TM program's beneficial role in the field of health.

A medical student whom I instructed in the practice of the TM technique said the following to me after taking the initial instruction, "I did not want to tell you this before, but I've had a heart murmur for many years. Now it is gone." At my suggestion she had her improved health verified by her doctor. When I saw her two years later she commented that she was still feeling great.

Here are some comments made by fifteen executives of a major Fortune 100 United States corporation after just *four* days of the Transcendental Meditation program.

> I've been meditating for four days now and the results have been much more positive than I thought they would be. I've been needing less sleep and feel more rested when awake. Also, I seem to have more energy, especially in the evening. My normal routine has been to settle in and watch TV after dinner. I've been doing less of this, feeling more inclined to participate in other activities ... In my work, I am feeling more inclined to take on a disagreeable task which I normally have a tendency to 'put on the back burner.'

1. I am sleeping deeper and requiring less sleep.
2. I am more alert — particularly in the A.M.
3. I feel more confident.
4. I am less irritable.
5. I have more energy following TM in the P.M.
6. I feel an overall calmness.
7. I feel a brotherhood with this group.
8. I like myself more.

I enjoyed the instruction far beyond my expectations. I found I had little trouble from the onset with the mechanics ... It has been many years since I have felt as moved by any experience as I have this last week with the TM practice. I am delighted, excited, and wish to thank you. Thank you.

TM is a beautiful way to release tensions. Since I have been meditating (4 days), I have not had a headache. For me, this is wonderful. I usually have headaches that last for days, however I have not had one since my initiation into the program. (If this is any indication of what is to come I can only say that no matter what the price it is 'well' worth it.)

At this juncture, there is no question but that I enjoy a deep sense of physical relaxation while meditating. I have experienced a slower rate of breathing and upon ending the meditation, a feeling of being 'ready to go' ... I am pleased with the almost immediate results which seem to have occurred in my case and am happy that I made the decision to begin TM. I am convinced that TM has immediate and long range application and fully intend to convince my wife to begin TM. Thanks.

I realize that this TM course will not only benefit me in this one phase, but throughout my life in all phases.

1. Have been averaging 1½ to 2 hours less sleep the first two nights and, though missing a night of meditation, last night woke up after 4½ hours of sleep refreshed and ready to get up. However, I went back to sleep for three more hours when I realized it was only 2:30 A.M.
2. Have awakened more refreshed after sleeping less.
3. Have noticed more interest and energy after *more* wakeful hours.
4. Have found that my speech and thought process are as quick or quicker but more deliberate and possibly sounder.

5. Seem to smoke (cigars) somewhat less and feel further reduction is coming.
6. Have found a general feeling of more happiness.
7. Have found a decrease in my appetite.
8. Pulse rate has dropped 20 points.
9. Have found my handwriting is more deliberate and clear.
10. Have found myself listening more effectively.

This course has been very beneficial for me. I feel that TM was something I had been looking for for some time...

Because the idea was not new to me, I was never uncomfortable with it. Due to a personality conflict in connection with my job, I anticipate that this is a successful means to help me.

Yesterday I functioned completely on two hours of sleep the night before. I feel TM helped me here. Stress situations this week (and I've had more than my share) haven't upset me to the degree that this caused any behavior that upset family life.

It is very refreshing.

My overall reactions are: it's the best practical ... most simple ... least demanding experience I've encountered in many years.

I've been through sensitivity training, T-groups, encounter groups ... the works ... But this simple process has more wholesome benefits than any of the above.

To understand how the TM technique is so effective in establishing and maintaining good health we first need to understand the cause of poor health. Disease is lack of ease. Lack of ease creates stress and weakens a person's natural defenses. Stress is the number one killer in the world. Medical professionals claim that stress is the underlying cause of virtually all health problems. In Chapter V, we saw how the TM technique produced a physiological state of rest that is more profound than deep sleep. Rest is directly opposed to stress. Rest eliminates stress. Deep rooted stress accumulated over many years requires deep profound rest to uproot and dissolve the stress.

Physiologists and psychologists agree that the mind and body are interrelated; if you affect the mind you will produce some corresponding effect within the body, and vice versa. A person reads some shocking news and the body chemistry immediately changes. Listen to a sweet melody and the body settles down. Shove somebody and a

Reversal of the Aging Process

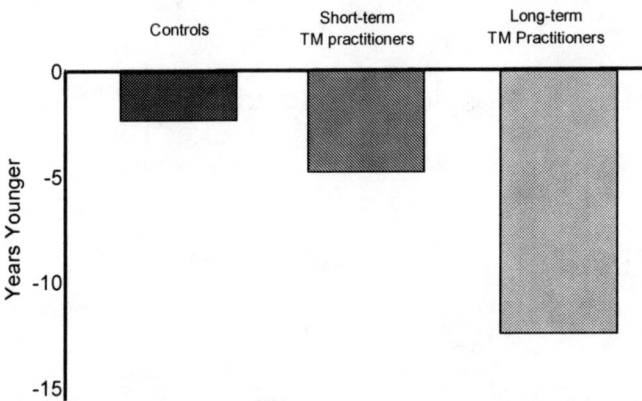

Fig. 11. Researchers testing the effects of the TM technique on the biological age of people—how old people are physiologically compared with chrono-logically—discovered that as a group, persons practicing the TM technique for less than five years were physiologically five years younger than their chronological age, as measured by lower blood pressure, better near-point vision, and better auditory discrimination. The group of long-term practitioners of Transcendental Meditation (over five years) were physiologically twelve years younger than their chronological age. This study was statistically controlled for variables such as diet and exercise.

References: 1. *International Journal of Neuroscience*, vol. 16, 1982, pp. 53-58.
2. *Journal of Personality and Social Psychology*, vol. 57, 1989, pp. 950-964.
3. *Journal of Behavioral Medicine*, 1986, pp. 327-334.

variety of associated thoughts are immediately triggered. Lie down at the beach and the mind drifts off on some pleasant reverie.

During the TM practice, as the mind experiences thought at increasingly finer levels, mental activity becomes less and less. With decreasing mental activity physical activity automatically becomes less. Finally, when the mind experiences the finest level of thought and transcends thought, to experience that wholeness of life where there is no impulse of activity — which is a common experience during the TM practice — the body gains a very deep profound rest.

Experiments show that this deep profound rest is unlike any state of rest that can be achieved during sleeping, dreaming or waking states of consciousness, and that this deep rest cannot be induced by hypnotic or operant conditioning methods. This unique state of rest resulting from the practice of the TM technique is what restores balance to the body and mind and enables one to maintain youthful health and vitality free from anxieties, worries and tensions. See Figs. 11, 12 and 13.

Decreased Hospitalization and Doctor Visits

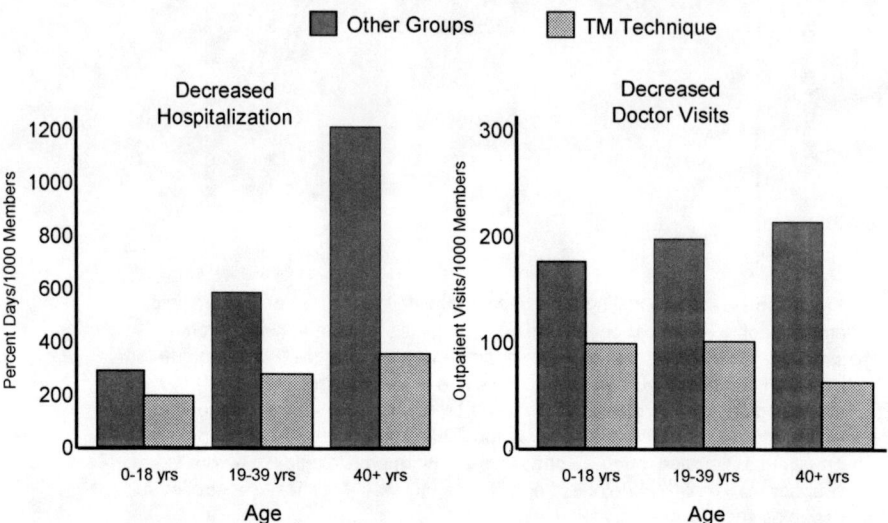

Fig. 12. A five-year study on 2,000 people throughout the United States who practiced the Transcendental Meditation technique showed that in comparison to the norm the TM practitioners had 56% less hospital admissions in all disease categories, including 87% less hospitalizations for cardiovascular disease, 55% less for cancer, 87% less for nervous disorders, and 73% less for nose, throat and lung problems.

References: 1. Psychosomatic Medicine, vol. 49, 1987, pp. 493-507.
2. *American Journal for Health Promotion*, 1996.

A salesman who practices Transcendental Meditation has renewed vitality after each vigorous day's work, is free from fatigue and stress, and is able to enjoy the evening with family or friends, or perform additional work if desired. Salesmen who practice the TM technique do not cope or live with stress. They live free from stress and fatigue. They enjoy a more productive life. They do not procrastinate.

We have seen in the preceding chapter how the TM technique increases the salesman's ability to think, speak and act efficiently. This

Reduced Anxiety

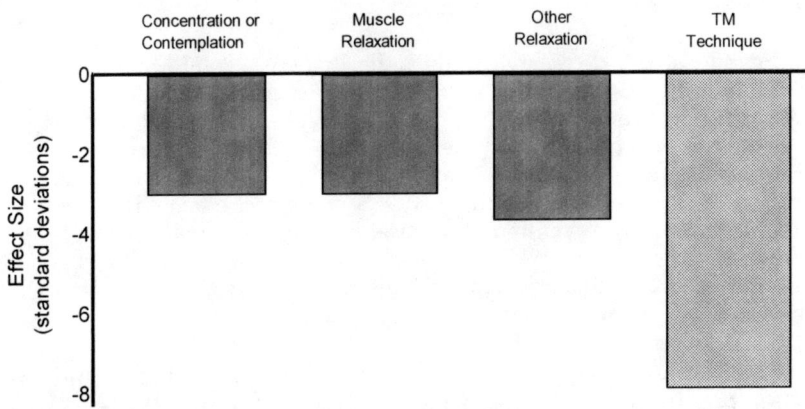

Fig. 13. A meta-analysis conducted at Stanford University of all of the 146 available independent studies showed that the Transcendental Meditation program as a means of reducing trait anxiety was statistically far superior than concentration and contemplation techniques or forms of physical relaxation, including muscle relaxation. Analysis indicated that these positive results could not be attributed to subject expectation, experimenter bias, or quality of research design.

References: 1. *Journal of Clinical Psychology*, vol. 45, 1989, pp. 957-974.
2. *Journal of Clinical Psychology*, vol. 33, 1977, pp. 1076-1078.

brings fulfillment in activity. Tensions, misery, suffering and failures in life come from an inability to fulfill desires. When desires are fulfilled fatigue and stress do not accumulate. The salesman leads a healthy, happy, productive life.

Dr. Nancy Lonsdorf (general practice, Washington, D. C.), says: My patients notice that their health complaints are exacerbated by stress incurred at work and at home. I tell them that the TM technique is the most effective, scientifically validated procedure to reduce stress and promote health. Of all the things they can do for their health, this has the most far-reaching, wide range of benefits. Hundreds of my patients have learned the technique—with excellent results. Every company should provide the TM program to their employees to reduce stress, help prevent disease, and promote good health.

And Hari Sharma, M.D., FRCPC, Professor Emeritus, Former Director of Cancer Prevention and Natural Products Research, Department of Pathology, The Ohio State University College of Medicine, stated:

> In many published research studies, the Transcendental Meditation technique has been shown to be the most effective technique for reducing stress and rebalancing the biochemicals in the body to produce improved physical and mental health. This has been corroborated by research showing that practicing of the TM technique reduces health care utilization by 50%. Because of the benefits of the TM program for prevention of disease, I recommend that it be covered by all health-care providers. In that way we can prevent forthcoming disorders that are extremely costly — not only financially, but also in terms of human pain and suffering.

If there were ever a new scientific discovery that could be acclaimed as the magic elixir of life, the TM technique deserves that distinction. The vast amount of empirical and scientific evidence supporting the role of the TM technique in improving and maintaining good physical, mental and emotional health cannot be ignored.

So for sales' sake meditate!

Chapter IX

Conquering Emotional Inhibitors

One of my first jobs after college was manager of field engineering for a leasing company in New York City. I needed to rush-order ten special multimeters which were manufactured by a small electronics company, say, XYZ Co., in Chicago. In response to my inquiry XYZ sent their salesman, Don, to see me. Don, I estimated, was in his late fifties, maybe early sixties. He wore a wrinkled plaid suit, and appeared to be insecure. I called on one of our engineers to sit in on the sales demonstration. As Don began his pitch I heard a strong clicking sound. At first I thought it was coming from the device Don was demonstrating. Then I realized that the clicking sound was coming from Don. His false teeth were sporadically chattering. They were not fastened well and when they chattered they looked and sounded like the novelty-gag false teeth that you wind up and place on someone's desk to get a few laughs. Don might have done okay on the Gong Show, but did not belong in sales. I had mixed emotions. I really felt for Don and at the same time I had to do all I could to restrain myself from laughing — it was that funny. He obviously maintained his job through nepotism. Don's problem was not so much his teeth. He was just so scared that his jaw trembled so hard that his teeth rattled. Don got his order, although I cannot credit him with making the sale. XYZ Co. had the product we needed and could make immediate delivery. This was the only reason we bought from Don. XYZ Co. was in a unique position. It manufactured a product which had no competition. Once other firms began to produce a similar product, Don's fear surely robbed him of his sales.

Dr. Hans Selye, renowned authority on stress, states that fear is physiologically harmful. In extreme cases stress caused by fear can result in destruction of the cells in the heart. There are cases on record of persons who literally were scared to death.

Emotional inhibitors are the greatest liability in selling. Fear is one of the biggest inhibitors to successful selling. Some other emotional inhibitors are:

insecurity	pessimism	rationalization
arrogance	depression	guilt
slovenliness	cowardice	inconsideration
unwillingness	moodiness	inattentiveness
nervousness	worry	mendacity
drunkenness	prejudice	absurdness
anxiety	dominance	deception
inferiority	immorality	inhibition
uncertainty	superiority	distrust
laxity	egotism	neuroticism
hypochondria	immaturity	insensitiveness
dependence	cynicism	abusiveness
impatience	neglect	inexpedience
enmity	gluttony	vulgarity
resentment	indifference	discontentedness

This is only a partial list. There are hundreds of emotional inhibitors which have a negative influence on selling.

Emotional inhibitors and their positive counterparts are the characteristics that make up personality. Webster's dictionary defines personality as "the complex of characteristics that distinguishes an individual ... the totality of an individual's behavioral and emotional tendencies." We can see that personality encompasses numerous variables. It is everything that we are including how we look, act, react, speak, gesture, etc.

Sales trainers know, as any salesman can also attest, that negative personality characteristics act as inhibitors to successful selling. Emotional inhibitors restrict the naturalness of selling. Experience tells us

Decreased Tobacco, Alcohol and Drug Abuse

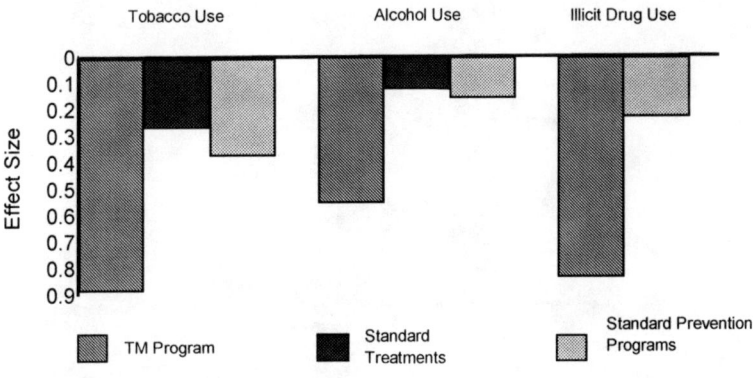

Fig. 14. A review and statistical meta-analysis of 198 independent studies indicated that the Transcendental Meditation program is uniquely effective for the treatment and prevention of alcohol, tobacco and drug abuse.

References: 1. *Alcoholism Treatment Quarterly*, vol. 11, 1994, pp. 13-87.
2. *International Journal of Addictions*, vol. 26, 1991, pp. 293-325.

that the less emotional inhibitors a salesman has the better he will be able to sell. A wholesome, pleasant personality is essential to the livelihood of the salesman. I will venture a guess and say that most salesmen have their share of negative personality characteristics with which they constantly battle to improve themselves and enjoy greater success in their highly people-oriented vocation. In an attempt to minimize the sales-inhibiting personality characteristics and to bring out the salesman's positive personality traits, sales trainers have produced hundreds of books, cassette tapes, training aids, gimmicks, and paraphernalia. As was mentioned earlier, many sales trainers also advocate theatrics, canned presentations, memorization of responses, cued speech inflections, facial expressions and body movements, positive-thinking exercises, pep talks, etc. All these types of methods mask over the problem, disguise it, may modify it, but do not resolve it.

Take, for example, the case of a "rehabilitated alcoholic." Can he take one or two social drinks and stop? Very unlikely, because the inner weakness which caused the alcoholic to drink has been sup-

Improved Psychology

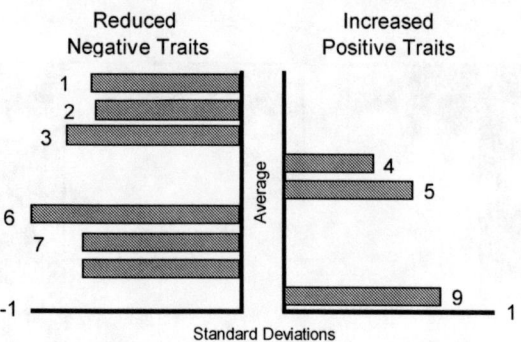

Fig. 15. Test results from administering the Freiberger Personality Inventory to 47 people practicing the TM technique between 4 and 11 years indicated marked improvement in 9 personality traits compared with a nonmeditating comparison control group.

Reference: *Scientific Research on Transcendental Meditation: Collected Papers*, vol. 1, 1974, pp. 420-424.

pressed and not removed. Unless that desire to drink is resolved and dissolved it will continually haunt the so-called rehabilitated alcoholic, waiting to surface as soon as his guard is down.

Psychoanalysts know that if the inner weakness is not resolved, but instead is suppressed, that inner weakness will find expression in another way. We all know of the person who stops smoking by sheer will power, but who then finds a new effect with which to deal, that of gluttony or nervousness.

In contradistinction to all other methods of personality development the TM program is par excellence because it dissolves the very deep rooted causes of emotional inhibitors.

Negative personality traits are due to the lack of contact with one's own inner nature. The solution to a problem never lies at the level of the problem. We must rise above the problem. No amount of analysis or manipulation of darkness will eliminate the darkness. What is necessary is to bring in light, and by virtue of bringing in light, darkness automatically disappears. Likewise, to resolve a deep-rooted problem, such as any of the emotional inhibitors, all that is necessary is to connect the salesman with his own "inner light." Connect the salesman with his own inner *self*, that full potentiality of life, that state of perfect orderliness, that field of inner life that is experienced as perfect silence, inner peace and happiness. By virtue of having one's awareness established in this field of *being*, which is the source and light of life, all forms of negativity, to include emotional inhibitors, are dispelled. They are dispelled because, when the mind is established in the field of perfect orderliness, all of our thoughts, speech and actions become attuned to the laws of nature. And nature, we know, is evolutionary and life-supporting. Therefore, only those personality characteristics of ours that are life-supporting will remain. All that which is not life-supporting will be dispelled, without the need for analysis, self-inquiry, positive thinking, etc. See Figs. 14 and 15.

This purification is accomplished naturally and spontaneously through the practice of the TM technique. Is this too good to be true? Not at all.

To understand this purifying phenomenon of the TM technique we can again draw a parallel comparison between physics and consciousness. The Third Law of Thermodynamics states that when the temperature (activity) of a given system is reduced its entropy (disorder) is reduced. During the practice of Transcendental Meditation the mind experiences thoughts at increasingly finer levels, i.e., at levels of decreasing mental activity. EEG measurements have shown that this produces orderliness in the functioning of the brain. When the mind transcends the finest thought to arrive at the home of all the laws of nature maximum orderliness results. When that state of awareness is established in our normal thinking, through the regular practice of the TM technique, there is no room for any disorderly emotional characteristics that are not in harmony with nature.

An experiment will illustrate the mechanics of the Third Law of Thermodynamics. A scientist freezes a beaker of salt-water. As the water freezes orderliness occurs; the water which had molecules randomly moving all around, now in ice form, has the molecules arranged in an orderly fashion. Moreover, as the temperature of the water is reduced to freezing, the salt in the water automatically separates out. Purification of salt from the water occurs spontaneously.

By similarly eliminating emotional inhibitors the salesman's positive personality characteristics remain. By being connected deep within his inner self, which is the source of nature itself, the salesman behaves in a natural, spontaneous manner. This is personality development!

Independent studies were performed on prisoners at Folsom Prison, California, Stillwater Prison, Minnesota, La Tuna Federal Penitentiary, Texas, Lompoc Federal Correctional Institution, California, and McNeil Island, a federal penitentiary in Washington. Repeatedly, it was found that prisoners practicing the TM technique showed significant growth of healthier mental attitudes and improved behavior compared to nonmeditating control groups.

If the TM technique can resolve and dissolve such deep-rooted psychiatric and behavioral personality disorders, certainly it can dissolve the more surface-level emotional inhibitors of salesmen. When emotional inhibitors dissolve, a natural, spontaneous wholesome personality results.

You will not have to remind yourself to feel happy—you will be happy. You will not need to remember to look sincere—you will be sincere. You will not have to stage confidence—you will be confident. You will not have to pretend to be interested in others—you will be genuinely interested in others. You will not pretend to act friendly—you will be friendly. You will not have to force yourself to work hard—you will apply yourself to your work out of the success and joy that your work brings you. You will not have to program yourself to think positive—you will be positive and therefore you will think positive. Procrastination and other bad work habits will automatically melt away, replaced by an energetic, positive work attitude. You will not have to memorize a canned pitch or a script of carefully phrased answers to clients' objections, and you will no longer feel it necessary to manipulate your clients—your thought, speech and actions spontaneously will be correct for any given set of circumstances. You will be aggressive—not abusive. You will be connected to that inner source of your own *being*, and that inner light will radiate outwardly as a glowing vitality. You will radiate a magnetic positivity and a command-presence that will automatically draw attention to you when you enter a room—this is the ultimate way to "dress" yourself for success. Also, with your expanded vision you will be more sensitive to each selling situation, and therefore will clothe yourself more appropriately for each selling circumstance. You will not have to tell yourself that you are terrific in order to build your self-esteem—you will be terrific and therefore self-esteem will be your natural status. As a natural outcome of your holistic personality development you will be confident. How can you not be confident when you have so many positive personality characteristics working for you? You will not need to perform a song and dance routine, or listen to pep talks in order to feel enthusiastic—you will be enthusiastic. By virtue of being enthusiastic you will feel enthusiastic. How can a confident, happy, energetic, successful, friendly, self-actualized salesman not be enthusiastic? You will gain mastery over yourself and your emotions, and with advanced study in the TM-Sidhi program you will even gain mastery over the laws of nature. You will not have to think of being in control of the selling situation. Your status and self-control will bear its own influence—you will naturally have control.

Above all, you will be natural. You will be yourself. You will not need to imitate, or force upon yourself, some top producer's selling style. You will be a top producer with your own natural style which others will try to emulate. When you naturally possess positive personality attributes and behave in a natural easy spontaneous manner people will want to do business with you. They will go out of their way to seek you out. They consciously may not know what draws them to you. Nevertheless, subconsciously they will be drawn to you like a magnet is drawn to iron. They will relate to your basic unforced, natural simplicity.

The holistic personal unfoldment resulting from the regular practice of the TM technique promises to create a new breed of salesmen, which is an essential requirement as we move into the 21st century.

By now, you probably have noticed that I make no attempt to tell you how to sell. Hundreds of books, tapes, and numerous selling aids already serve that purpose. Rather than creating another book on sales methodology I preferred to show you how you can develop the basic foundation which is essential to any and all selling situations, i.e., how to contact *being* and allow your natural inner self to spontaneously work for you. Therefore, this book gives you what no other sales book provides: an insight into the mechanics of holistic personal unfoldment. With a holistic personal unfoldment for a foundation, you will *naturally* sell like you have never sold before.

For sales' sake meditate!

Chapter X

Creating a Happy Home Life

Freedom from emotional inhibitors is the basis for a happy home life. The quality and strength of the home life is determined by the quality and strength of the individuals who comprise the family unit. Marriages and families, for the most part, have been a compounding of individual problems. As long as individuals are tense, worried and unfulfilled they will radiate that influence around them. This negative influence is what contaminates and destroys close family interpersonal relationships. The divorce epidemic we have been experiencing the last decade echoes the discontent within individuals.

The key to permanent harmony and happiness in home life lies in having permanent harmony and happiness established within individuals. The key to permanent happiness in individuals is in the understanding that there are two fields of life; the inner, absolute, nonchanging field of life, and the outer, relative, ever-changing field of life.

The outer, relative, ever-changing field of life is in a continuous state of transition. Therefore, it is not possible to experience permanent happiness in that field of life which is transitory by nature. For permanent happiness we must look to that which is permanent, nonchanging. To understand this nonchanging field of life we draw a parallel to quantum mechanics in physics. We have seen that this permanent, nonchanging field of life is the state of least excitation; itself nonchanging, but that which is at the basis of all changes. It is permanent, eternal, unbounded and beyond the limits of space and time. This state, we have also seen, is our own inner life.

That which quantum mechanics describes can be verified by direct experience through the practice of the TM technique. It is experienced as perfect silence, harmony, inner peace and happiness. This basic, inner, permanent level of life is where permanent happiness is to be found. It is only necessary to have your awareness anchored in this inner life. As a result, you will naturally imbibe that permanent inner peace and harmony into your very nature, and you will radiate that influence to others around you.

Established within your inner *being* you will maintain that inner stability of peace and happiness which will be unchallenged by the passing waves of vicissitudes in your life. You will not be ruled by your emotions. You will not overact, or react from an emotionally restricted perspective. With your awareness established at the source of change you will be master in the field of change, with permanent happiness as your foundation.

We have already seen how the TM technique dissolves emotional inhibitors. Deep-rooted selfish traits disappear. A natural flow of heartfelt compassion results. This is the foundation for a giving relationship.

To be most efficient at his work a salesman needs to have a happy home life. A salesman's energies should not be dissipated in discontent at home. The salesman's spouse (wife, in this example) is essential to his success. The wife is the focal point in the family. Therefore, meditation is, at least, of equal importance for the wife. The salesman meditates for a few minutes at the office before coming home. As a result, he loses the fatigue and stress of the day. The commute back home is more enjoyable. When he gets home he greets his wife and children with an open heart. He does not dump his day's problems on his family. Likewise, the wife who meditates before preparing dinner, frees herself from the frustrations of her day's work and prepares dinner with joy. Meanwhile, the children also meditate. When the family comes together for mealtime the whole atmosphere is enriched. The family enjoys their time together in peace and harmony.

Incidentally, the TM technique is very beneficial for children. Dr. Francis G. Driscoll, former Superintendent of Schools for Eastchester, New York, was one of the many school administrators who introduced the Transcendental Meditation program to junior and senior high-school students. Research studies support the following:

1. Students improve their grades.
2. Students get along better with teachers.
3. Students get along better with parents.
4. Students get along better with other students.
5. Evidence of lessening use of drugs.

Families who meditate together stay together. They grow and prosper together as a harmonious unit. Helen Yellin, mother of four sons, married for 47 years and meditating for 21 years, says,

> TM makes you more aware of the needs of your loved ones, and gives the energy and insight to meet those needs ... I would say to any woman, to any man, too, TM is the best investment you'll ever make in yourself, your relationship, your family.

Her husband, Jerry, 73, supports her sentiment; "Transcendental Meditation has made us stronger in ourselves and brought us closer together as a couple."

When considering a happy home life we need to go beyond the boundary of our immediate family. From a broader perspective the salesman's community is also his home. The strength of a community is based on the strength of the family. The community can only be as strong as the collective strength of the families comprising the community. Family unity is the basic fabric of society.

When individual communities are living in peace and harmony with mutual respect and compassion for one another, then, the entire nation comprised of all the communities is strong and peaceful. A nation is only as strong as the combined strength of the communities which comprise it. When there is social unrest, even in any one part of a nation, the entire nation suffers.

Responsible leaders of society have realized that the peace, power, prosperity, happiness and success of a community are based on the collective peace, power, prosperity, happiness and success of all the constituents of the community. In their search for a means to improve the community by improving the individual, leaders have inquired into the merits of the TM program. Once convinced of its merits, leaders have publicly stepped forward to introduce the TM program to society.

Twenty-five years ago Thomas P. Salmon, then governor of Vermont, sent a letter to every legislator in Vermont, every school superintendent and principal, every social service agency and to many state employees urging them all to personally investigate the TM program as a means to utilize our most abundant and yet untapped natural resource: man's inner potential of energy, intelligence and creativity. Also at that time, the governors of Illinois, Maryland, Nebraska, Washington and Wisconsin issued proclamations to encourage their respective constituents to use the TM technique to improve the quality of their lives. Likewise in 1972, the Illinois House of Representatives passed a resolution strongly encouraging the statewide implementation of the TM program in order to uplift society as a whole.

Due to the efforts of these individuals, and others like them, the TM technique has gained increased acceptance in society over the last three decades. At this writing almost one percent of our nation has begun the practice of the TM technique.

When we consider the need to strengthen the community in order to strengthen the nation, we must also consider the business community. The salesman's community is not only his place of residence, but also the place of his business. At work he lives and interacts with his community of business associates. The individual is the building block of a corporation. A corporation is only as strong and successful as the collective strengths and successes of the people who work for it. For maximum corporate growth collective harmony needs to exist. Collective harmony is orderliness in action—efficiency. Efficiency is the intelligent application of energy. An efficiently run company maintains orderliness, even amidst chaos.

A company structured with individuals who are anchored deep within themselves, who are connected to the source of life itself, who have energy, intelligence and wisdom, whose actions are in attunement with the underlying laws of nature, will naturally grow in success and prosperity because nature moves in the direction of success and abundance. Success and abundance is the natural evolutionary flow of life. When workers are in tune with nature then the collective output of the corporate community of workers must yield success and prosperity.

Gil Younger, president of Transco, a manufacturer of replacement auto parts, credits the TM program for his firm's 299% profit growth in five years. He reported that the annual increase in profit directly correlated to the annual increase in the percent of employees meditating in his firm. He notes that the 299% profit growth is mostly due to increased productiveness since payroll has increased only 34%. His company's growth rate exceeded expectations in spite of fuel problems, reduced auto usage and service, and inflationary pressures. Younger states:

This did not happen from any high-powered, production, manage-ment, or sales meeting, or psych sessions or banners and slogans. It just happened, spontaneously and easily. After fourteen years in business we are amazed to find such a simple and inexpensive pro-gram that dramatically improves productiveness while generating harmony and cooperation ... I certainly recommend Transcendental Meditation to all companies that want improved progress. Subjec-tively I must say, 'It is a pleasure.'

The strength of an entire nation depends upon the collective strength of its people. When people are living happy, prosperous and fulfilled lives the family unit is happy, peaceful and prosperous. A collection of happy, peaceful and prosperous families results in a har-monious and prosperous community. When each and every residen-tial and business community is living in harmony, peace and prosperity, then the entire nation is strong and powerful. Therefore, the status of a nation is a reflection of the collective status of each and every individual. Everyone has the responsibility to his nation, and that responsibility is to uplift oneself. To uplift oneself it is only neces-sary to connect one's awareness to that inner source of life itself. We have seen how this will result in peace, power, love, success and pros-perity in daily life. The nation will then reflect that collective status of its constituents.

It is only when individuals are at peace within themselves that the nation can be peaceful. When each nation is at peace within itself then we will see peace throughout the world. World tensions, conflicts and wars are due to the collective dissatisfactions of individuals. There-fore, the only solution to world peace is through the fulfillment of individuals. The TM technique, by bringing one's awareness to that absolute fullness of life within, enables each individual to also have fullness in the outer field of active life. This creates a happy home life—and home is inclusive of one's immediate family, one's residen-tial and business community, one's nation, and the world.

You as a salesman have a greater influence in society, America, and the world than you may realize. The salesman is the pivot point in industry. Therefore, it is the salesman who can make the greatest impact on the progress of our nation. The wheels of progress would stand still were it not for salesmen. The best engineered and manufac-tured products benefit no one until they are sold. Ideas are a dime a dozen and meaningless until they are implemented. Before they can be implemented they must first have had to be presented to someone—they had to be sold. The best of services benefit no one unless there is a sales effort to bring the service to the awareness of consumers. Even as great an invention as the telephone, which was initially ridiculed, had to be sold to the public. The entire field of banking and finance would be stagnant were it not for salesmen negotiating contracts, investment vehicles, finances and services.

Selling is the oldest, most basic sustaining force of public and private enterprise. Professional services of lawyers, doctors and even health and social services of nonprofit organizations, normally not thought in terms of being sold, are often communicated by word of mouth based on the goodwill generated by staff and administrators incorporating salesmanship. All interactions between individuals involve salesmanship. Today's news is sold to the public. Even the clergy, realizing the impact of salesmanship, incorporate salesmanship into their sermons and services. Educators use salesmanship to sell youngsters knowledge. Therefore, it is the salesman, who by practicing the TM technique, can make the greatest possible contribution to his community, to his nation and the world.

This is not some fanciful theoretical dissertation, but a practical achievable reality in this generation because, all that is necessary is for just one person in one hundred to meditate. One percent of the people in society, company or nation is sufficient to bring about a positive influence within that society, company or nation.

To test this concept of "1 in 100," two researchers, Dr. Candace Borland and Garland Landrith III studied the effect the TM technique had on restoring order to one of the more negative behavioral aspects of society: crime. All cities in the United States with a population of over 25,000 were studied for their crime rate. Every city in the United States that reached one percent of the population meditating showed a marked decrease the following year in the crime rate as reported in the Uniform Crime Reports compiled by the Federal Bureau of Investigation. Additional studies are being conducted to measure other effects on society where one percent of the people are practicing Transcendental Meditation. See Fig. 16.

The 1 in 100 phenomenon should not be surprising since this principle is found throughout nature. In physics, a one-percent alignment of the electrons in a magnet is sufficient to maintain the strength of the whole magnet. In biology, the orderly functioning of an entire cell is caused by the orderly functioning of DNA which constitutes less than one percent of the cellular material. In laser mechanics, stimulated light emission by one percent of the atoms is sufficient to produce macroscopic wave coherence resulting in laser light. In chemistry, a supersaturated solution requires just one additional crystal to create an orderly crystallization of the entire solution. In neurophysiology, the orderly functioning of the entire brain results from less than one percent of the brain cells functioning orderly.

The TM technique opens one's awareness to the home of all the laws of nature where maximum orderliness is found. This produces a concentrated orderly life-supporting influence within the individual resulting in more productive activity, happiness and prosperity. This positive influence of a few people practicing TM is sufficient to bring an orderly life-supporting coherence to the functioning of the entire community. Only one percent of the people practicing the TM technique is necessary to bring about a phase transition (transformation) in the community, work environment, nation and the world.

Dr. Ronald David who is the Chief Medical Officer of Washington, D. C. General Hospital, and former lecturer in public policy with John F. Kennedy School of Government, Harvard University, stated:

> An impressive body of scientific research indicates that practice of the Transcendental Meditation technique by a small proportion of a population reduces stress and creates a positive influence in the entire population. This means that employees in a company practicing this stress-reduction modality will not only benefit the company, but should have far-reaching benefits for the larger society as well.

Since the salesman holds a prominent role in the success or failure of America as a nation, it is up to the salesman to take the initiative and become a leader by taking control of himself. Begin the practice of the TM technique, draw on your inner resources, unfold your full potential, and enjoy a happy, peaceful, prosperous and successful life. This role of leadership will be the positive influence that you will radiate wherever you go. This is all that can be expected of anyone. This is living a spiritual life. It is said that spirituality is not correct belief, but righteous (right action) living. We already saw how right action is achieved. As one's consciousness expands through the practice of the TM technique, he becomes more aware of the truths of his own religion. The TM technique is a simple mechanical procedure which enhances the spiritual growth of the individual.

Rev. Joseph M. Occhio stated in his letter to the editor of the Beacon newspaper:

Decreased Crime Rate

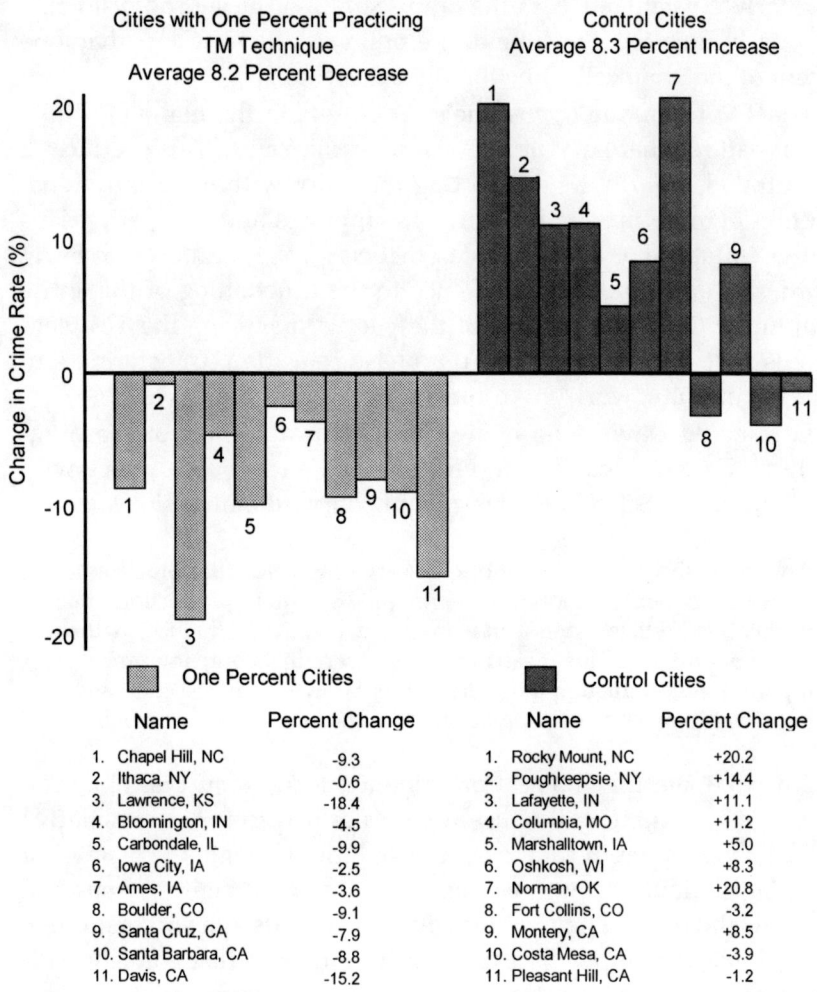

Name	Percent Change		Name	Percent Change
1. Chapel Hill, NC	-9.3		1. Rocky Mount, NC	+20.2
2. Ithaca, NY	-0.6		2. Poughkeepsie, NY	+14.4
3. Lawrence, KS	-18.4		3. Lafayette, IN	+11.1
4. Bloomington, IN	-4.5		4. Columbia, MO	+11.2
5. Carbondale, IL	-9.9		5. Marshalltown, IA	+5.0
6. Iowa City, IA	-2.5		6. Oshkosh, WI	+8.3
7. Ames, IA	-3.6		7. Norman, OK	+20.8
8. Boulder, CO	-9.1		8. Fort Collins, CO	-3.2
9. Santa Cruz, CA	-7.9		9. Montery, CA	+8.5
10. Santa Barbara, CA	-8.8		10. Costa Mesa, CA	-3.9
11. Davis, CA	-15.2		11. Pleasant Hill, CA	-1.2

Fig. 16. Eleven cities in which at least one percent of the population had learned the TM technique were studied from 1972 to 1973, compared with 11 matching control cities with relatively few meditators, but otherwise comparable in population, location, and crime statistics. Crime decreased an average of 8.2 percent in the one-percent cities and increased an average of 8.3 percent in the control cities; a total variance of 16.5 percent.

References: 1. *Scientific Research on Transcendental Meditation: Collected Papers*, vol. 1, 1974, pp. 639-648.
2. *Journal of Crime and Justice*, vol. 4, 1981, pp. 25-45.

Yes I am a priest and a meditator. Why did I get involved with TM? Because I found it to be a happy conclusion to a long personal search ... Briefly, the essentials of TM can validly coexist with Christianity. You can be a good Catholic and a practicing meditator. Try it. You will like it.

Raphael H. Levine, Rabbi Emeritus of Temple De Hirsch Sinai, stated in his May 1, 1975 letter of support for TM:

Since I have been meditating I have often been asked how TM relates to my Judaism. I have discovered no conflict to my faith as a Rabbi nor to any religion which I have studied. On the contrary, its undoubted benefits in increasing one's mental and physical energy can only help people appreciate their own religion more by relieving the mind and the nervous system from the inevitable stresses of life. Thus it helps a person to a more wholesome and healthy mental attitude, which our respective faiths teach is the way to achieve fullness of life ... It can only enrich our appreciation and sensitivity of the great values of our respective faiths.

Reverend Dr. Craig Overmyer (meditating 25 years), a pastoral counselor in Indianapolis, Indiana, who holds a doctorate of divinity said:

I decided to commit my life to Christ after I'd been practicing the Transcendental Meditation program for three months ... I would say to any Christian—to anyone of any religion—that the TM program would benefit your life. It's a technique, a simple process that requires no belief. It is not a religion.

Rabbi Alan Green (meditating 23 years) of Beth Israel Synagogue in Winnipeg, Manitoba states:

The Transcendental Meditation program has made me a better rabbi because it has given me an experience and insight into the profound depths of life ...

Reverend Leo James Hoar, Director of Notre Dame High School, stated in his January 7, 1974 letter of support for TM:

However, upon learning more about Transcendental Meditation ... I realized that it in no way conflicted with my religion or belief of God, but actually complemented it ...

In conclusion, I would like to recommend the practice of Transcendental Meditation as a means of creating a more peaceful world and enjoying life more fully in the spirit of rest and strength, awareness and growth.

The collective effect of one percent of the people in America meditating will result in a phase transition that will spiritually regenerate our nation. By meditating you are making the greatest contribution possible to yourself, your family and your nation. It is up to the salesman, who has the greatest impact on society, to do his share to bring about this phase transition. Then, we will live the ideals upon which this nation was built. America will become strengthened by each of its individual constituents to fulfill the destiny with which it has been endowed — to be one nation, under God, indivisible, with liberty and justice for all. This will be a happy home life, indeed!

For sales sake meditate!

Chapter XI

Your Seven Steps to Success

A Brief Summary

The preceding text illustrates the holistic development derived from the practice of the TM technique. To the uninitiated, hearing of the many benefits resulting from the practice of a simple mental technique may create a credibility gap. Individuals who have not begun the practice of the TM technique cannot help but doubt and wonder how such a simple technique can produce such a wide range of benefits in so many facets of one's life. To summarize: the TM technique connects you to *being*, that basic nurturing inner essence of life, your own inner 'self.' By contacting this inner value, which we can also call "pure creative intelligence," all outer aspects of your life will flourish. Connect with your inner self, gain nourishment from within, and health, wisdom, success and happiness will be yours spontaneously and naturally.

This same principle is seen in the growth of a tree. By watering the root we enable the tree to be nourished from the basic level of the sap, and this nourishment spontaneously and naturally develops all facets of life in the tree; its leaves, stems, branches, buds, bark, trunk, etc.

Because of the holistic benefits derived from the practice of the TM technique, the TM technique is being recognized as a major scientific discovery in human development. As a salesman, whose livelihood depends on the level of your personal development, you cannot afford to be without this simple sales training tool. The TM program makes the pep talk, manipulation and theatrical presentation types of sales development obsolete. Old schools of thought will produce old ways of doing things and old results. Developing salesmen to make full use of their mental potential is one effective way to meet the challenges of our times. The TM technique achieves this.

There are many philosophies and organizations that embrace the truths expounded in this book. However, no other school of thought offers the *technique* for realizing the truths expounded in such a systematic, simple and direct manner, except for the TM program. There are many techniques available in the marketplace which produce various beneficial results. But none that I have studied—and I have done thirty years of research in this field—other than the TM technique, *connects* you to your inner infinite *being*, and therefore produces holistic beneficial effects. If I knew of another shortcut to personal development I would have included it in this book. In Maharishi's words,

> Transcendental Meditation opens the awareness to the infinite reservoir of energy, creativity, and intelligence that lies deep within everyone.
>
> By enlivening this most basic level of life, Transcendental Meditation is that one simple procedure which can raise the life of every individual and every society to its full dignity, in which problems are absent and perfect health, happiness, and a rapid pace of progress are the natural features of life.

Experience Is Necessary

I did not write this book as a philosophical dissertation on a new sales training concept, but rather, to provide salesmen with an introduction to the *practice* and *experience* of an advanced sales training method. In order for knowledge to be complete, both the intellectual understanding and the experience are necessary. Experience is the best teacher. How complete is knowledge without experience? How is it possible to explain the experience of sight to a person blind since birth? A blind person has only the experience from the senses of hearing, taste, touch and smell from which to draw an inference. The sense of sight, however, is too different from the other senses for the blind person to be able to know what sight is on the basis of intellectual inquiry and inference from his other sensory experiences. At best, a blind person could conceptually appreciate the benefits of seeing. He intellectually would know that with sight he would not bump into things, he could move faster, be able to catch a ball, etc. However, a few seconds experiencing sight will do more to teach the heretofore blind person about sight than could be achieved in a lifetime of intellectual inquiry about sight.

The TM technique opens your awareness to a new state of consciousness, transcendental consciousness. Physiologists have determined this state to be unlike the waking, dreaming or sleep states of consciousness. How is it possible, then, to communicate verbally what transcendental consciousness is to persons who only had the experience of waking, dreaming and sleeping states of consciousness from which to draw an inference? It is not possible. Experience is necessary. Short of the experience, the best that can be done is to discuss the benefits that result from the experience of transcendental consciousness. However, discussing the benefits will not produce the benefits. The proof of the pudding is in the tasting.

Fortunately, the TM technique is easily learned in seven basic steps.

Seven Simple Steps

The first step in learning the TM technique is to attend an introductory lecture which takes about one and one-half hours to complete. The introductory lecture explains what the TM technique is, presents the latest in scientific research findings about TM and discusses the benefits to be derived from its practice. An introductory lecture provides you with the opportunity to ask questions and to discuss various points with the instructor. Introductory lectures are given free of charge at TM centers throughout the United States and internationally. In-house company lectures are also made available.

The second step, a preparatory lecture, is also about one and one-half hours long, and usually follows the first step within a week's time. At this lecture the mechanics of how and why the TM technique works is discussed in detail. Questions are answered, and an opportunity for enrolling in the program is provided. Preparatory lectures are also free of charge.

The third step is taken at the conclusion of the preparatory lecture. It is the time for enrolling into the TM program. It consists of a short ten-minute interview with the instructor.

The first three steps are all that are necessary to prepare for learning the practice of the TM technique. The next four steps take about two hours each and are completed over four consecutive days.

The fourth step is personal instruction. It is given on a one-to-one teacher-to-student basis. After learning the TM technique the student practices on his own for a while, then meets with the instructor to discuss his new experience. The student then meditates at home as instructed and returns the following day for the fifth step.

The fifth step is group instruction. Additional knowledge is provided. The procedure for correct meditation is verified. There is also the opportunity for discussing one's experiences and reviewing the benefits that are already being noticed from the previous practice sessions at home.

The sixth step is also in the context of group instruction. Correct practice is verified. The mechanics of the TM technique are reviewed and additional intellectual knowledge is provided to complement the experiences resulting from the daily TM practice sessions at home.

The seventh step is also in the context of a group meeting. Correct practice is verified. At this meeting additional intellectual knowledge of the mechanics of developing higher states of consciousness, beyond the fourth state of consciousness is provided. The group meeting is followed by a brief private review with each student. A wholesome graduation atmosphere prevails, and a feeling of brotherhood is experienced within the group.

Lifetime Membership

Checking – The seventh step is not an end, but a beginning of a lifetime membership in the TM movement. In order to assure that the practice is being done correctly, meditation *checking* sessions are provided. The first checking session is in a group meeting and is scheduled ten days following the seventh step. Correct practice is verified, meditation experiences and the benefits realized from the practice of Transcendental Meditation are discussed, and a thorough review is made of all material covered in prior instruction. The meeting lasts approximately two hours. At the conclusion of this meeting all course participants are encouraged to make appointments for periodic personal checking sessions.

Personal checking is a one-to-one meeting with an instructor to review the correctness of the student's TM practice. Periodic checking assures that the TM practice is continued correctly and that maximum benefits are being realized. Personal checking meetings, which last about one-half hour, also provide the opportunity for the meditator to have his questions answered. There is no limit to the number of personal checking sessions that a person may attend.

Advanced lectures — As one's personal growth is enhanced the thirst for more knowledge grows. To meet this need a weekly series of advanced lectures is conducted. Correctness of practice is verified and questions are answered. Audio or video-taped lectures are provided which cover a wide range of material relating to the personal growth experienced by meditators. These group meetings last about one and one-half hours. There is no limit to the number of advanced lectures that a person may attend.

In-House Sales Training Programs

The TM program is also available within the context of an in-house corporate sales training program. These programs are tailored to fit the needs and tight schedules of executives and salesmen. No program is too big or too small to implement. The Maharishi Corporate Development Program consists of 10 in-house seminars, including instruction in the Transcendental Meditation technique, two personal consultations with each participant, and an optional two-day in-residence seminar. In addition to this 18-hour program for executives, a shorter 12-hour program is offered for salesmen. An optional continuing program is recommended to maximize participation and long-term benefits.

> The secret of success in business today is to develop the field of creativity that lies deep within each individual. This Corporate Development Program provides the technology through which the awareness of the individual comes into contact with pure consciousness — the field of unlimited creativity, which is the total potential of Natural Law. The spontaneous result of this regular experience is that the infinite dynamism and organizing power of nature are made available in daily life. Application of this technology will ensure that the goal of business, which is to bring prosperity, progress, and fulfillment to individuals and society as a whole, is achieved.
>
> Maharishi

Live 200% of Life

By enrolling in the TM program you will begin to gain the benefits and will personally validate the claims which have been presented in this book. The TM technique is an experience. Without the experience your knowledge about the TM program is not complete.

Here is a simple procedure whereby you gain everything you want in the outer field of life by systematically diving into the inner field of life. You can live 200% of life—100% inner and 100% outer—simultaneously. This is fulfillment in life.

The TM program is there for the taking. Do not pass up this opportunity.

For sales' sake meditate!

Part II

Advanced Training

The TM-Sidhi Program

Chapter XII

The TM-Sidhi Program

The wisdom of utilizing full mental potential is not new. It has its roots in ancient history. It has been recorded in the oldest continuous tradition of knowledge on earth, the Vedic tradition of India. Maharishi has brought to light this ancient Vedic knowledge. According to this Vedic tradition, pure Transcendental Consciousness is the underlying field of natural physical laws. It is the most fundamental level of nature itself, which modern day physics has discovered to be the grand unified field of all the laws of nature. This pure Transcendental Consciousness is also the most fundamental level of the mind, and contains the full creative potential of the mind. By following certain prescribed mental procedures while maintaining awareness at the level of pure Transcendental Consciousness — the home of all the laws of nature — it is possible to utilize basic physical laws to spontaneously achieve effects of extraordinary superhuman magnitude. Different procedures produce different effects. The series of procedural formulas that are identified in the Vedic literature, in Sanskrit, are called *siddhis*, and pronounced 'sid-heez.'

Essentially, siddhis are techniques which enable one to make full use of one's mental abilities. There are many siddhis recorded in the Vedas, about one thousand to be more exact. Some are so mind-staggering that were I to include them I felt that it would be so far beyond the conditioned thinking of many readers that it would be incomprehensible and may cause readers to dismiss this entire book as imaginative fancy. Therefore, I have intentionally not mentioned specific abilities.

I do not expect you to believe that supernormal abilities are part of every person's latent potential. However, you owe it to yourself, at the very least, to accept the *possibility* that these abilities might be part of your natural birthright.

The first step to achieving anything is knowing that it is within the realm of possibility. As long as people felt that it was not possible for heavier-than-air objects to fly, an airplane could not be built. Believing otherwise, the Wright brothers built an airplane and flew. At first, they did not fly far, they did not fly high, and they did not fly for long. But they flew. Once you accept the possibility of accomplishing something you are well on your way toward achieving it.

Almost everyone has had some personal experience that appeared to extend beyond the limits of the senses. Perhaps it was a spontaneous knowledge that a friend was about to telephone, and just then the friend called. Have you ever felt very familiar in a place where you have not been before? Did you ever have a dream that came true? Did you ever know intuitively what someone was going to say just before they said it? Are such experiences to be looked at as freaks of nature, or are these hints of potential abilities? They are hints of potential abilities.

How does a moderately-built judo expert take his relatively weak hand and plough it through a stack of bricks that would resist breaking by a hefty construction worker using a sledgehammer? Does the judo expert accomplish this feat by how he positions his hand at the point of impact with the bricks? Or is it how he holds his mind at the point of impact with the bricks? Experts claim that the bricks shatter as a result of applied mind power; that the hand follows the force of the mind which acts as the leading edge for the hand.

Extraordinary feats of strength have also been exhibited by persons reacting spontaneously in emergency situations. I recall a news account of a person manually lifting a truck to free a person pinned beneath it, later bewildered at how he was able to lift such a heavy object. Such accounts are not that rare.

Consider also, the "bona fide" psychics. Are they freaks of nature? Or are they just tapping their latent potential?

One psychic lady I am aware of has the uncanny ability to predict earthquakes. She registers her predictions with the United States Geological Survey in Denver, Colorado. She claims to be about 85% accurate in forecasting where the earthquake will strike, when it will strike, and how strong it will be. She says that she predicts earthquakes in the hopes that her demonstrations of accurate predictions will open people's minds to accepting unusual mental abilities.

On January 3, 1981, to prove her precognitive abilities, she broadcast over a radio station that an earthquake measuring between 3 and

3.4 on the Richter scale would occur in the vicinity of Los Angeles on either January 7th, 8th, or 9th. The following Thursday morning, January 8, Los Angeles was moderately shaken by an earthquake that officially measured 3.2 on the Richter scale. Its epicenter was two miles southwest of Malibu Beach.

One correct prediction can be dismissed as a lucky guess. Repeated correct predictions must lead one to consider that maybe events cast their shadows before they occur, and that perhaps some people are sensitive enough to be able to perceive these shadows.

Like child prodigies born with talent, some persons are born with certain supernormal abilities, while other persons occasionally have spontaneous experiences of one or more superhuman powers. (By now, you must realize that I use the terms *superhuman* and *supernormal* lightly. These abilities are all part of our normal range of functioning.) Now, however, it is possible to systematically unfold full use of one's mental potential in order to utilize the latent faculties of the mind, nothing being left to chance.

In 1977, newspapers in Canada, Europe and the United States carried articles about the new breakthrough in human potential announced by the TM movement. The announced breakthrough was not so much a new discovery of human potential, but rather, a breakthrough in the ability to understand full human potential in terms of modern-day quantum physics. What heretofore furrowed eyebrows and challenged comprehension is now readily discernible under scrutiny of even the most meticulous of scientists.

The news report included information about a special course of study structured by Maharashi, which he called the "TM-Sidhi program." The TM-Sidhi program is a natural extension of the Transcendental Meditation program and may be learned after two months of regular practice of the Transcendental Meditation technique. Practice of the TM-Sidhi program accelerates the progress of the individual towards realizing his full potential — the state of enlightenment.

The daily practice of the Transcendental Meditation technique opens the awareness to Transcendental Consciousness, the home of all the laws of nature, which is the basis of everyone's awareness. It is on this deep inner level of awareness that the TM-Sidhis are practiced, thereby culturing one's ability to think and act from this level. By learning to function from this deep inner level of awareness, which is the home of all the laws of nature, the mind gains support of nature for the fulfillment of desires. With the TM-Sidhi program, thought and action spontaneously become more in accord with the evolutionary power of natural law. This results in greater skill in action and the ability to fulfill one's desires naturally.

The siddhis which are taught by the TM-Movement accelerate the development of higher levels of intelligence, learning ability, creativity, and neurological efficiency. Of particular interest is instruction in one aspect of the TM-Sidhi program called "Yogic Flying," the preliminary stage of levitation.

Only when the individual has developed sufficiently in his practice of the Transcendental Meditation technique whereby he can maintain his awareness at its simplest level in Transcendental Consciousness will the person be able to gain command over the laws of nature and successfully perform the siddhis. It is from that fine level of consciousness where one experiences directly the unified field of all possibilities that anything is possible. And *anything* means even levitation.

Physicist Dr. John Hagelin explains:

> Yogic Flying, the ability of the body to float and fly really demonstrates mastery over the gravitational force. And you can't master gravity without transcending the classical laws that prevent such a phenomenon. That means without taking recourse to quantum gravity. And quantum gravity, again, is the level of the unified field. So Yogic Flying is a clear, clear demonstration of the capability of the human nervous system to function coherently at the level of the unified field.

The ability to levitate or even to fly, has been a recorded heritage of humanity in Europe, Africa, India and Australia. In *Butler's Lives of Saints* over 200 saints are reported to have levitated (Thurston & Attwater, 1962). Also, according to legend, one sect of Buddhist monks locks its neophyte meditator into a sealed room with only an out-of-reach window available for an exit. The monk remains there in isolation, brought only food and drink, until he floats out of the window (graduates) and joins his peers.

There is not much more that I can say about the TM-Sidhi program. Listing the specific techniques that are taught and providing the method of performing the techniques is intentionally beyond the scope of this book. It is important that this special program of study be made under close supervision. The TM-Sidhi program harnesses our principle power: the mind. It is important that we have absolute control over it. It is important that the techniques for the unfoldment of mental potential are taught in safety and in a context which will assure that such techniques are not misused. It would be foolish and irresponsible to teach someone to drive a car by giving them the ignition keys and sending them for a solo drive in the mainstream of highway traffic. Driving is simple, but there is a set procedure to do it. An orientation to driving is necessary. The mechanics of driving, some safety procedures, and knowledge of how the controls work should first be reviewed. Then, some experience of driving while under supervision is necessary. Likewise, the simple practice of unfolding one's mental potential is learned.

It is important to emphasize that the TM movement does not teach the control or manipulation of others. The TM program and the TM-Sidhi program are concerned with personal unfoldment, not mastery over others, but mastery over oneself—self-unfoldment. This is the basis for achieving success in life. Success does not come from attempting to dominate, control or manipulate others. Such are the causes of failures.

You can approach the challenges of business and personal life from a limited perspective and with limited use of your resources, or you can draw upon that latent infinite reservoir within your inner self. You can meet the challenges of life from a fully developed status. Why, then, limit yourself to anything less than full use of your mental potential. You were endowed with this powerful resource. Use it.

For sales' sake meditate!

Chapter XIII

Experiencing Levitation

In 1978 I was extremely fortunate to have been able to attend a six-month-long intensive research study into consciousness as the field of all possibilities conducted by MERU in Switzerland. About 1,800 people from 37 countries attended this special study. Among the enrollees were some of the world's most distinguished and respected scientists. The primary disciplines represented were physics, biology, physiology, medicine, sociology, education, management, agriculture and psychology. Most enrollees, such as myself, were there for personal development, but also served as research subjects.

We were separated into smaller, more manageable groups and located in many rented hotels around the city of Interlaken. Men and women had their separate accommodations, except married couples who were housed at the couples' accommodations. The group I was in consisted of 186 course participants. Batteries of psychological and physiological tests were administered with extensive EEG studies made to log brain wave activity before, during and after the performance of various siddhis. Of particular interest was the study of the phenomenon of levitation.

When the time came for us to receive instruction in how to levitate, none of us really believed we would do it. I knew intellectually that levitation was humanly possible. But could I do it? I have to admit that, although I hopefully anticipated being able to levitate, my doubt that I would really levitate was very strong. I believe that this feeling was shared by most, if not all, of the other participants. After we received instructions in levitation, called "Yogic Flying" by our instructors, we were all to come together as a group the following day for an actual practice session with our instructors. I could not wait to get to the meeting hall the following morning.

Next morning, when I entered the hall, I realized that when we were told by our instructors that we would do Yogic Flying they must have been serious since the meeting hall was made devoid of all chairs and furnishings, and was lined, wall-to-wall, with eight-inch-thick foam rubber padding. The room quickly filled at the appointed time with all of us anxious doubters. We sat scattered around the room and began practicing as instructed. Almost immediately the instructors shot up off the foam. Then, like popcorn popping, students throughout the room began lifting off. There was much laughter and expressions of joy as people lifted off the foam. As I continued with the practice I suddenly felt a surge of buoyancy accompanied by a feeling of bliss. And up I went. The experience was momentary. There was a slight forward thrust during the hop and I came down about three feet in front from where I lifted off. Then, up I went again, and down I came. And up again, and down again. Boing! Boing! Boing! With each lift-off I experienced a momentary hovering and a great feeling of freedom as I broke away from the pull of gravity. It was very exhilarating to say the least. During my college years I was a member of a skydiving club. My experience of Yogic Flying was much like the experience of weightlessness I had when I reached terminal velocity during skydiving. However, instead of the accompanying adrenalin surge I had in skydiving, I experienced bubbling bliss as I popped around the room doing my Yogic Flying practice.

Initially, there was some traffic congestion and a few minor accidents as we haphazardly sprung up into the air in all directions. After the initial novelty of the Yogic Flying experience we instinctively learned control and maneuvers; right turns, left turns, and no arms or legs flaring during lift-offs. The group organized itself quickly and we were now "Yogic Flying" around the room in an orderly fashion. Guys were racing each other around the room, playing tag and having a grand time with their newly discovered ability.

"Hey guy, this sure beats jogging!" one fellow exclaimed as he bounded past my left shoulder making a perfect landing in the foam several feet in front of me.

"Show off," I retorted. Then, I easily thought of the Yogic Flying instruction, determined to beat him. Boing, boing, boing, boing, boing — I spontaneously and without effort, just by mental intention, made a thirty-foot series of hops leaving him well behind. Like the Wright brothers, we did not fly far. We did not fly very high. Neither did we fly for very long. But we flew.

There are various stages of Yogic Flying. The initial stage is "hopping." The second stage is "floating," and the final stage is "flying."

The unfoldment of these stages is dependent upon the extent to which a meditator is able to sustain his awareness at the level of the unified field, the level of Transcendental Consciousness, that most fundamental level of life where all the laws of nature reside. It is by maintaining one's awareness at this very fine level that one is able to influence the laws of nature to gain support of those laws whereby anything is possible. That is why the unified field is called the field of all possibilities; from that most fundamental and powerful level anything is possible.

A sequence of photos depicting Yogic Flying is on display at local Transcendental Meditation centers. Also, a thirty-minute color videotape called *Yogic Flying* is available from Maharishi University of Management Press, Fairfield, Iowa 52557-1115. Maharishi is joined by world famous magician Doug Henning, Dr. John Hagelin, Dr. Keith Wallace, and Dr. Bevin Morris in explaining how Yogic Flying takes place and its profound benefits for the individual and society.

The ability to levitate or perform any of the other superhuman abilities is not abnormal. It is the result of the unfoldment of one's normal faculties. Persons who lack full use of their mental potential look upon the more highly developed individuals with astonishment and awe, and label such highly developed individuals as "superhuman." The reality is that anything less than full normal use of mental potential is subnormal. The label "superhuman" is a relative one. What is considered extraordinary today will surely become average and commonplace tomorrow. Have we not seen this occur throughout recorded history? The consciousness of the masses always trails that of the few advanced thinkers in society. Today every elementary school child takes for granted the common knowledge that was considered to be the most profound and advanced thought of yesterday.

Years ago only a few daring thinkers had the courage to proclaim that the earth was round, not flat. Also, initially, only a few persons dared to state the earth revolved around the sun. Not long ago almost everyone knew for sure that it was not possible for man to build a flying machine. And just two years before our nation landed a man on the moon newspapers reported statements by some scientists that a manned trip to the moon was impossible. They said we could not build a spaceship large enough to carry the amount of lead shielding that would be necessary to protect the lives of the astronauts from the radiation belt through which they would have to pass. Repeatedly, myopic schools of thought have been shattered by the leadership of the advanced thinkers of their time. Progress goes on in spite of the inertia of the conditioned thinking of the masses.

How is the TM-Sidhi technique, Yogic Flying, applicable to the field of sales? The intent, of course, is not to develop light-footed salesmen who float into their clients' offices, or who take shortcuts by flying out of tall buildings to their parked cars below. The Yogic Flying and other TM-Sidhi techniques have a serious application in selling as you will discover in the next chapter. How creative are you? Based on what you have read in this book thus far, can you think of how the practice of Yogic Flying and other superhuman abilities have a practical application in your sales profession? The following statement by Maharishi provides a hint:

> The performance of siddhis, which in the days of ignorance were termed superhuman powers, is not something superhuman. Everything is within the normal range of man's ability. To handle the whole of cosmic life is within the range of everyone's own nature, because it is the same nature ... Until now the philosophy of fulfilling desires was to struggle ... Now we have to awaken mankind to a new philosophy of life ... I am reminded of a successful businessman in America sitting with his eyes closed, who proclaims success in his activities by closing the eyes and practicing the Transcendental Meditation technique. This is the changed face of success. Success lies in handling nature, and nature is one's own nature. The more you are able to handle yourself, the more you are able to handle the world.

See the point?
For sales' sake meditate!

Chapter XIV

Why Practice Yogic Flying?

Let us look at some of the reasons why salesmen should be practicing the TM-Sidhi program. The application of developing higher levels of intelligence, learning ability, creativity, and neurological efficiency are obvious and need no comment. But, of what value to the sales profession is the practice of Yogic Flying? There are several reasons.

First, the practice of the TM-Sidhi techniques is fun to do. Take, for example the Yogic Flying technique. I personally find it tremendously revitalizing. I can be completely beat from a vigorous day's work, but, after practicing Yogic Flying for a while I am recharged and raring to go. It is a very pleasurable experience, and one characterized by a feeling of freedom as the bondage of gravity is released. It is also a social function. Fellow Yogic Flyers get together at the local TM center, put on their jump-suits and do Yogic Flying.

Second, the practice of superhuman abilities is a test of our personal growth. The practice of the TM technique and the TM-Sidhi technique enables one to contact the home of all the laws of nature, and through regular practice, to structure the home of all the laws of nature in one's awareness. Hence, a highly developed mind-body coordination is achieved. It should be possible, then, for meditators to verify their personal growth by levitating by mere intention. The performance of siddhis is, in effect, a feedback indicator of our progress.

Third, studies conducted at Maharishi European Research University, researching consciousness as the field of all possibilities, disclosed that EEG brain-wave coherence was maximum during the time siddhis were being performed. The greatest brain-wave coherence was evident when the Yogic Flying siddhi was being practiced. It is the performance of the Yogic Flying siddhi, then, that has been determined to be the best means to bring maximum orderliness to the functioning of the brain. Concurrently, at the point of lift-off, when brain-wave coherence was maximum, physical activity was at its peak. Where the TM technique develops wholeness of awareness in Transcendental Consciousness, the Yogic Flying siddhi best develops the ability to maintain that level of Transcendental Consciousness in an active state. See Fig. 18.

Optimizing Brain Functioning through the TM-Sidhi Technique

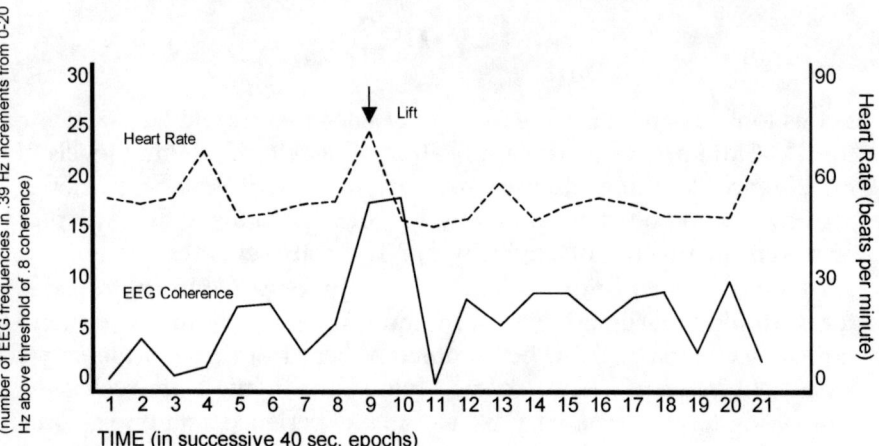

Fig. 18. Studies at Maharishi European Research University disclosed that the ability to maintain Transcendental Consciousness, as measured by its physiological correlate, EEG brain wave coherence, increased during the practice of TM-Sidhi techniques and was maximum when lift-off occurred during the practice of the Yogic Flying siddhi. This indicates that the practice of the TM-Sidhis, especially the Yogic Flying siddhi, optimizes orderliness in the functioning of the brain. Concurrently, at the point of lift-off, when brain wave coherence was maximum, physical activity, as measured by increased heart rate, was also at its peak; a state of perfect functioning of mind-body coordination was evident. Hence, practicing the TM-Sidhis, with emphasis on the Yogic Flying siddhi, develops the ability to maintain the level of Transcendental Consciousness (the field of all possibilities) in an active state, which enables fulfillment of desires by mere intention.

References: *Scientific Research on Maharishi's Transcendental Meditation and TM-Sidhi Programme: Collected Papers*, vol. 5, 1990, pp. 3574-3596.

It is the Yogic Flying siddhi that produces the greatest linkage between Transcendental Consciousness and activity, that is, the greatest coordination between mind and body. Hence, the practice of the Yogic Flying siddhi is the means to accelerate the development of one's mind-body coordination. In other words, wholeness of consciousness grows fastest with the practice of the Yogic Flying siddhi.

This is the primary reason for practicing the TM-Sidhi techniques, with emphasis on Yogic Flying. They are not performed for the purpose of accomplishing a few remarkable feats, but to serve as a means to create a permanent link of Transcendental Consciousness in dynamic activity. It is when Transcendental Consciousness is able to be maintained, fully established concurrently in dynamic activity, that fulfillment of any desire is enabled.

It is said that man is born in the image of the Creator. Man is the microcosm duplicate of the macrocosm universe. "As above, so below," is the great axiom. All of the powers and the laws of the universe are also found within man. We are the embodiment of total natural law. Not understanding this fact and not knowing how to tap the full potential of natural law within us, these fundamental laws of nature, the powers of nature, lie dormant. It is analogous to a man, who being unaware of the huge inheritance left for him by his father, believes himself to be poor. Unaware of his wealth he does not use it. He continues to live in poverty. Someone finally comes along and tells him of his inheritance. His awareness gets connected to the bank and he receives a simple procedure whereby he can tap and utilize his vast wealth in the market. Instantly, he no longer is found to suffer from poverty. Nothing has changed in this man's life, only his awareness of his own status and the knowledge of the procedure necessary to use his resources. Likewise, in considering superhuman powers, there is nothing to attain or acquire. You already have everything as your natural birthright. You only need to become aware of your status and learn how to contact that field of all possibilities, that field of pure potentiality, that territory of natural law, within you and apply it in your daily activity in order to achieve maximum success from your actions.

> The TM-Sidhi practices give us a habit; they create a habit in us to function from the least excited state of consciousness, which is the field of all possibilities. And functioning from the field of all possibilities means we materialize our desires quickly.
>
> Maharishi

Persons using only a limited, surface level of their minds find expression in a limited arena of speech and action. The practice of the

TM-Sidhi techniques extends the range of mental functioning by actively utilizing the Transcendental Consciousness state of consciousness in activity, thereby serving to deepen and extend the sensory-motor channels to their utmost extent.

Earlier it was mentioned that according to Vedic tradition, and now verified by physics, Transcendental Consciousness (pure consciousness, Cosmic Mind) is not only the source of thought, but also the generator of all physical manifestations and events throughout nature — consciousness is not just a local phenomenon in the brain. By bringing one's individual mind in attunement with cosmic mind whatever one desires immediately begins to happen. Any intention of the mind at that basic level of natural law must become a phenomenon in the obvious world.

Continued practice of the TM-Sidhi techniques stabilizes our ability to function from the field of all possibilities. When the ability to function from the field of all possibilities is fully stabilized, it is called *enlightenment*. The successful performance of siddhis, therefore, is a test of, as well as an accelerating influence in, the growth of enlightenment in our consciousness. The ability to perform superhuman feats is inseparable from enlightenment. Enlightenment is living the wholeness of life; living one's life with awareness structured in the home of all the laws of nature (individual mind in complete attunement with cosmic mind.) With awareness structured in the home of all the laws of nature one gains maximum effectiveness in every action.

Maharishi states:

> Action is always based on the level of consciousness. A man can only see red when he has red glasses on, and then he cannot see anything other than red. In the same way, when we raise a person's level of consciousness, he can only behave rightly. An ideal society will result from people's spontaneous right behavior, which will take within its fold all the necessary considerations for the proper sense of values for their own interests and for the interests of other people. An ideal society can never be created by telling people the importance of caring for the interests of others. A balanced life can only grow in society when every action is spontaneously able to accommodate both the interests of the individual and the interests of those around him, and this will be on the basis of his ability to perform action that is spontaneously in accordance with all the laws of nature. Only action in accordance with nature will simultaneously satisfy the interests of the individual, society, and the cosmos.

FOR SALES' SAKE MEDITATE!

Finally, the effect produced by a group practicing their TM-Sidhis together is far-reaching. We have seen in our prior considerations of quantum physics how a small number of atoms in perfect phase with one another create a synergy of coherence throughout the entire structure. Quantum physics refers to this phenomenon as *super-radiance*. Likewise, the principle of super-radiance occurs when a group of individuals practice the Yogic Flying technique together. The collective group practice produces an orderly harmonious effect throughout the community through the omnipresent nature of consciousness itself. Remember, from earlier discussion, that consciousness may be likened to the omnipresent quantum field. Hence, the quantum field of omnipresent consciousness is capable of influencing and correlating events without localized limitations. An excerpt from Dr. Byron Rigby's paper presented at the 1977 Sixth World Congress of Psychiatry in Honolulu, Hawaii, explains:

> When individual consciousness is focused, its influence is localized to the object of attention and to the individual observer. However, when focal attention is allowed to become unbounded, as in the Transcendental Meditation technique, then individual consciousness is continuous with collective consciousness. As consciousness approaches its state of least excitation, larger and larger areas of collective consciousness are included in the individual's awareness. It is for this reason that Maharishi has insisted for many years that it is the transcending process itself which confers the primary benefit on social organization, and not simply the improved productive output of the individual's daily activity.

On this basis we can see how a few individuals within the sales department of a corporation, who meditate and practice the TM-Sidhi techniques, will not only achieve greater success for themselves, but will, through the omnipresence of collective consciousness, produce an orderly, coherent, and harmonious effect in the productivity of other nonmeditating employees around them as well—the entire corporation benefits. Through the combined efforts of a few individuals in a corporation practicing Yogic Flying it is possible to enhance the success quotient of the entire corporation.

Corporate leaders and sales trainers are beginning to realize that it is now possible to create a group of salesmen who have the field of all possibilities open to them through the development of consciousness, and thereby, they can create, through the super-radiance effect of collective consciousness, an ideal corporation; one characterized by orderliness, harmony, efficiency and successful right action. But do not wait for others to take the initiative for your personal development. You take the initiative.

For sales' sake meditate!

Chapter XV

An Invitation to Enlightenment

The world is undergoing a change unprecedented in history. No stone is being left unturned and no individual is being unaffected. You are seeing the changes taking place around you and in your own life, and you undoubtedly are noticing that the tempo of the changes, in all avenues of life, has been accelerating at a dramatic rate. What you are witnessing is a phase transition, a radical reconstruction phase where the evolutionary force of progress is moving at an exponentially accelerating rate. The old is phasing out as the new is being superimposed in its place. We are in an exponential curve of a scientific age where scientific achievements in all fields are phenomenal. What were topics for science fiction a few years ago are becoming a part of our daily accepted reality.

Part of this phase transition is the awakening of human consciousness. The Transcendental Meditation and TM-Sidhi programs are playing a paramount role in precipitating this awakening of consciousness.

In 1958 Maharishi brought to the world the ancient Vedic knowledge of how to unfold full use of one's mental potential. As Maharishi traveled around the world offering the simple TM technique, thousands of people from all walks of life responded by enrolling into the TM program. By word of mouth news quickly spread — astonished by the results of their new practice, meditators encouraged their family and friends to join in. This was the beginning of a global awakening of consciousness.

Encouraged by the huge receptivity to the TM program, and to meet the growing demand, in 1972 Maharishi formulated a World Plan to train teachers of the TM-technique throughout the world and to establish one center for every million people in order to disseminate the knowledge and experience of unfolding higher states of consciousness in every community. By enabling everyone to unfold the full use of their mental potential and to utilize their infinite inner resources, peace, prosperity, creativity, good health, harmony and happiness is becoming the new way of life in the world.

As a trained physicist, Maharishi predicted that when one percent of the population practiced the TM technique, a phase transition would occur analogous to those seen in physical systems such as physics, chemistry and biology. (Please see Chapter X for a review of the principle whereby only a small number of individual components are needed to create orderliness and coherence in a structure.) Maharishi predicted that the experience of pure transcendental consciousness by one percent of the population would create a sufficiently strong collective effect of orderliness and creativity whereby the influence would radiate to all members of society. In this way all of society would be uplifted.

By the end of 1974 there was a sufficient number of cities in which one percent or more of the population was practicing the TM technique. Scientific statistical evidence supported Maharishi's prediction, and gave concrete evidence that, in fact, a phase transition did occur at the one-percent threshold level—negative trends in society decreased, crime rate decreased, accident rate decreased, overall health improved, positive trends in political life were noticed and even the weather and agricultural productivity improved. Repeated sociological studies by independent researchers in different parts of the world have collaborated the initial findings. In honor of Maharishi, the phenomenon of bringing about a phase transition in society when one percent of the population is practicing the TM technique has been named the "Maharishi Effect."

On January 12, 1975, inspired by the scientific research verifying that by unfolding individual consciousness in a fraction of the population of a society a phase transition can be brought about throughout the society, Maharishi inaugurated the Dawn of the Age of Enlightenment. In his inaugural speech on board the Flagship Gotthard, on Lake Lucerne, Switzerland, Maharishi said, "It is through the window of science that we see the Dawn of the Age of Enlightenment."

By the end of 1977, the Maharishi Effect was being experienced in almost 1,000 cities around the world where the threshold level of one-percent participation in the TM program had been reached. There were nearly two million people practicing the Transcendental Meditation technique in over 140 countries. The phase transition of the Dawn of the Age of Enlightenment had begun. To more rapidly advance this global phenomenon, Maharishi introduced the TM-Sidhi program, opening the door to even more rapid growth of mental development.

Continued scientific studies, numbering over 600 to date, have validated the influence of coherence being generated by the increasing number of people practicing the Transcendental Meditation and TM-Sidhi techniques (currently five million world-wide). It is ushering in a new age and creating a new paradigm of living where everyone is able to master the laws of nature at their source in pure consciousness, thereby living in happiness, success and fulfillment.

In 1997, to meet the expanding demand for its programs, a multi-billion-dollar world-wide Maharishi Global Construction program was initiated to build some 4,500 Maharishi Vedic centers throughout the world. Of highest priority is to build 450 of these centers in the United States — one for each Congressional District. These centers will house medical doctors who offer preventive medicine programs which will have the practice of Transcendental Meditation and the TM-Sidhis as a central theme. The architectural style of the buildings is based on Maharishi Sthāpatya Veda, the most ancient science of architecture and planning in accord with natural law, to promote health and prosperity. This architectural science includes such factors as site selection, proper positioning of buildings on their sites, proper dimensions and proportions of the buildings, proper placement of rooms, use of natural nontoxic building materials and energy-efficient construction.

The 21st century will be the age of the mind. It will be a time when everyone will be educated in the full use of their mental potential. We have already seen that full use of mental potential means enlightenment. When everyone is fully utilizing their mental potential, having the home of all the laws of nature established in their awareness, the entire society will be an enlightened society. As of this writing we are witnessing the Dawn of the Age of Enlightenment. We see a few advanced thinkers taking up the leadership role in developing full use of their mental potential.

We have seen that all that is necessary to develop full use of mental potential is to allow the mind to take a dive deep within itself, make contact with its infinite reservoir of energy and intelligence where the field of all possibilities and the home of all the laws of nature reside, and then, on that basis perform action. Action spontaneously will be right.

Action in accordance with the laws of nature is right action and must result in success and fulfillment in life, since nature does not make mistakes. Nature moves in the direction of fulfillment. When we are synchronized with nature, then we too must move in the direction of fulfillment. Remember, there is no chaos in nature. Everything in nature is harmonious. We may be in rapid change, but it is still harmonious. If things appear chaotic to you it is only because you are not in tune with the changes. When you are living in phase with the laws of nature you will experience peace, harmony, joy, success, wealth, and prosperity — all the laws of nature support you. If you are out of phase with the laws of nature you will feel pushed around. Ever try launching a boat out of phase with the incoming waves? You get battered around. However, when you launch the boat in synchrony with that same force of the waves, you get full support of the waves.

Irrespective of your present circumstances your greatest opportunity is here and now. Whenever there is a period of accelerated change there is the opportunity for accelerated personal growth. It is only a matter of being able to put yourself in synchrony with the progressive, orderly accelerated change that nature is undergoing.

I am reviewing these points which have been brought out earlier because they are crucial to understanding that you have free will and you can harmonize your will with that of almighty nature, or you can do otherwise.

There are two sides to any change. There is the evolutionary side, and there is the dissolutionary side. How well you harmonize with the evolutionary side depends upon how deeply you are anchored at the underlying cause of change, i.e., to what extent you have incorporated the home of all the laws of nature in your awareness. This will determine to what extent you are in synchrony with the immutable evolutionary laws of nature. Do not be like many people who allow themselves to be tossed about by the vicissitudes of life, then, in ignorance, blame outside factors and circumstances for their fate. Leading thinkers from all disciplines have realized the opportune times in which we are living and have seized this opportunity to develop themselves as citizens of the Age of Enlightenment.

Within the selling profession a new caliber of salesman is necessary to meet the increased challenges that lie ahead. It is the salesman who will need to lead his company through changing economic scenarios and intense competition. It is *you*, the salesman, who provides the sustaining force to private enterprise. It is the success of your selling efforts that are essential to the health, growth, and even survival, of your corporation. The salesman who begins the practice of the TM technique and who unfolds the use of his latent abilities through the practice of the TM-Sidhi techniques will have a tremendous advantage over those who do not have this special training. The advantage will not be from a manipulative posture any more than a sighted man takes advantage of the blind. It is just by virtue of having sight that the advantage exists. It is just by having this superhuman status that the advantage exists. No manipulation of others is intended, implied, desired or necessary.

Further, the new scientific age into which we are entering will be highly complex. Those persons who have developed themselves in the full use of their mental potential will be able to keep up with the changing times and will be in great demand. Those who do not follow up on the opportunity unveiled in this text will be losing out and wondering why.

Currently, tens of thousands of persons, on their own and through company-sponsored programs, are systematically unfolding their full mental potential. Progressive corporations, recognizing that harnessing and utilizing the mind is the greatest capital investment they can make for their future, are implementing TM programs as part of their regular staff training. You are already competing against supersalesmen. The unfoldment of the full use of one's mental potential is an exponential one, and therefore, there is no catching up. You need to join the silent ranks of meditators or be left far behind. Do not become lost in the pace of progress—time and tide wait for no man. The age of the supersalesman is here and now.

Ironically, many corporations, still living in the dark ages, will still try to improve their sales by the implementation of more gimmicks and hard-sell theatrics. But the consciousness of the buyer is also growing. Salesmen still running around armed with gimmicks and theatrics will be seen for what they are: adults who engage in childish folly. These salesmen will be missing sales and wondering why.

Supersalesmen are honest, sincere, friendly, enthusiastic, poised, confident, good-natured, happy, healthy, virtuous, have strength of character, and exemplify the qualities of love and compassion. They will have a path beat to their doors. Customers will seek them out in order to do business with them. Such will be the salesmen of the 21st century. They will emerge as the new top producers and leaders of corporate America.

There is not much more to say. I have found the practice of the Transcendental Meditation technique to be very meaningful in my life, and thereby, have fulfilled a lifelong dream. This book is my attempt to share my treasure trove with you. I hope that I have made you aware of your infinite potential as a human being, and I also hope that, at the very least, you will give the TM technique a try. Experience for yourself the benefits described in this book.

By the combined efforts of a few individuals it is possible to accelerate the Age of Enlightenment, rapidly bringing peace, love and brotherhood into every community, nation, and the world. This is not just an idealistic dream. It is the realistic realizable potential of the Transcendental Meditation and TM-Sidhi programs.

In closing, I echo Maharishi's invitation to you to become a citizen of the Age of Enlightenment:

> Good time for the world is coming. Now, a few people in any country will be able to change the destiny of their nation for all good. One percent of the population will be sufficient to design the direction of time for all happiness, progress, and fulfillment everywhere. I see the Dawn of the Age of Enlightenment. In this scientific age, it is no longer necessary for any nation to continue living with problems. This is the time of the dawn of the Age of Enlightenment. I am only giving expression to the phenomenon that is taking place. One percent of the people in any country can herald the dawn of a new age for the whole nation by devoting only fifteen minutes of their time twice a day. With such a little demand for such a great offer it is not conceivable that the world will go any longer in the footsteps of suffering. It is in the hands of a few individuals in every country today to change the direction of time and guide the destiny of their nation for all harmony, happiness, and progress. It is my joy to invite everyone to come in the light of the knowledge and experience that the Science of Creative Intelligence provides and enjoy participating in this global awakening to herald the Age of Enlightenment.
>
> Maharishi

For Sales' Sake Meditate!

Appendix A

Getting Started

To locate your nearest center for learning Transcendental Meditation:

Toll-Free: 1-888-LEARN-TM (1-888-532-7686)

http://www.tm.org

To inquire about corporate development programs:

Toll-Free: 1-888-624-2747

http://www.tm.org/mcdp/

Appendix B

Suggested Additional Information

A variety of books and videotapes about the Transcendental Meditation and TM-Sidhi programs are available from Maharishi University of Management Press. To obtain a free catalog call toll-free 1-800-831-6523. Website: http://www.mum.edu/press/

I recommend the following books:

1. Maharishi Mahesh Yogi, *Science of Being and Art of Living.*
2. Hari Sharma, M.D., *Freedom from Disease.*
3. Robert Keith Wallace, Ph.D., *The Neurophysiology of Enlightenment, How Maharishi's Transcendental Meditation and TM-Sidhi Program Transforms the Functioning of the Human Body.*
4. David F. O'Connell and Charles N. Alexander, *Self Recovery, Treating Addictions Using Transcendental Meditation and Maharishi Ayur-Veda.*

I recommend the following videotapes on Yogic Flying:

1. Dr. John Hagelin, *Physics of Flying.*
2. Maharishi Mahesh Yogi, Doug Henning, Dr. John Hagelin, Dr. Keith Wallace, Dr. Bevin Morris, *Yogic Flying.*

Additional copies of this book may be ordered by calling the publisher toll-free at 1-888-934-0888; inquire about quantity discount. Books may also be ordered from the publisher online at www.hatsoffbooks.com, or from other online booksellers, or by placing an order with your local bookstore.

About the Author

A Brooklyn-born Californian, Vincent Daczynski received his engineering degree from Utah State University. He began his career as a Field Engineer with IBM Corporation. He then joined LMC Data, quickly rising through the ranks to become National Manager of Field Engineering. In 1969, Mr. Daczynski left the business world to study full-time in India with Maharishi Mahesh Yogi where he became a qualified instructor of the Transcendental Meditation Program. He returned to the business world, taking a position with Singer Business Machine Company as product service manager, advanced systems, during which time he also established a Transcendental Meditation club for his colleagues.

Mr. Daczynski changed careers to stockbroker where he also made presentations on the TM program to fellow salesmen. Realizing the direct benefits of the TM program as a sales training tool, Vincent Daczynski developed his lecture notes into this highly useful book.

In 1972, Vincent Daczynski joined Maharishi University of Management where he worked for five years in various financial positions, taught the TM program part-time, and completed in-depth training in the TM-Sidhi program.

Subsequently, Mr. Daczynski joined the federal government to continue his career in finance as a budget and financial analyst. Retired from civil service, he now devotes his time teaching the TM program to businessmen.

Mr. Daczynski, who has authored a book on speculating in oil and gas leases, enjoys sky diving, traveling to exotic corners of the world, prospecting, organic gardening and strolling along the beach with his wife, Melinda. His daughter, Dawn, and his son-in-law, David, have given Vince three fine grandchildren: Joshua, Bethany and Janell.

LaVergne, TN USA
17 May 2010
182962LV00001B/293/A